THE NYIF
VEST-POCKET GUIDE TO
STOCK BROKERAGE MATH

THE NYIF
VEST-POCKET GUIDE TO
STOCK BROKERAGE
MATH

William A. Rini

NEW YORK INSTITUTE OF FINANCE

NEW YORK • TORONTO • SYDNEY • TOKYO • SINGAPORE

Library of Congress Cataloging-in-Publication Data

The NYIF Vest-Pocket Guide to Stock Brokerage Math /
    William A. Rini.
        p. cm.
    ISBN 0-13-847690-X
    1. Investments—Mathematics.   I. Rini, William A.
HG4515.3.R36 1992   92-32223
332.6′01′51—dc20   CIP

Printed in the United States of America

10   9   8   7   6   5

This publication is designed to provide accurate and authoritative
information in regard to the subject matter covered. It is sold with
the understanding that the publisher is not engaged in rendering
legal, accounting, or other professional service. If legal advice or
other expert assistance is required, the services of a competent
professional person should be sought.
*—From the Declaration of Principles jointly adopted by a
Committee of the American Bar Association and a Committee of
Publishers and Associations*

ISBN 0-13-847690-X

ATTENTION: CORPORATIONS AND SCHOOLS
NYIF books are available at quantity discounts with bulk purchase
for educational, business, or sales promotional use. For information, please write to: Prentice Hall Career & Personal
Development Special Sales, 240 Frisch Court, Paramus, NJ 07652.
Please supply: title of book, ISBN number, quantity, how the book
will be used, date needed.

NEW YORK INSTITUTE OF FINANCE
Paramus, NJ 07652

A Simon & Schuster Company

On the World Wide Web at http://www.phdirect.com

Prentice-Hall International (UK) Limited, *London*
Prentice-Hall of Australia Pty. Limited, *Sydney*
Prentice-Hall Canada Inc., *Toronto*
Prentice-Hall Hispanoamericana, S.A., *Mexico*
Prentice-Hall of India Private Limited, *New Delhi*
Prentice-Hall of Japan, Inc., *Tokyo*
Simon & Schuster Asia Pte. Ltd., *Singapore*
Editora Prentice-Hall do Brasil, Ltda., *Rio de Janeiro*

To **Catherine**...
  my GOOD wife
    my BETTER half
      my BEST friend

ISBN 0-13-847690-X

HOW THIS BOOK CAN HELP YOU

Solve Two of the Toughest Problems When Preparing for the "Stockbroker's Exam"

Those wishing to become licensed as stockbrokers must pass the series 7 examination. This exam, known officially as the "General Securities Registered Representative Examination," is very rigorous. Traditionally, students without a financial background have a difficult time with the mathematical calculations peculiar to the world of stocks and bonds. Many are also relatively unfamiliar with the proper use of the calculator, and are thus doubly hampered in their efforts to become registered.

This book helps you overcome both problems. *It not only simplifies the math, it also shows you how to make an effective tool of the calculator.*

Increase Control over Your Own (or Your Client's) Investments

Investors (and licensed stockbrokers) have the same problems. They need to know, for example:

- How much buying power there is in a margin account.
- What a portfolio is worth.
- How to read the newspaper stock listings.*
- The amount of accrued interest on a debt security.
- Whether a dividend is due to a stockholder.

*All exhibits are from *The Wall Street Journal.*

These and many other questions—all critical to successful investing—can be answered only by employing the proper calculations. While such skills are absolutely necessary for the stockbroker, they are also of inestimable value to the individual investor.

The NYIF Vest-Pocket Guide to Stock Brokerage Mathematics is therefore the book to have before and after taking the series 7 exam.

It covers all the mathematics you need to master to pass the exams for brokerage licensing and other NASD/NYSE licensing, including the series 6 (Mutual Funds/Variable Annuities), series 52 (Municipal Securities), and series 62 (Corporate Securities).

After the examination, it serves as an excellent quick reference when you need to make an important calculation right away.

HOW TO USE THIS BOOK

Each type of calculation is presented in a clear and consistent format:

1. The *explanation* briefly describes the purpose of the calculation, the reason for it, and how it is best utilized.

2. The *general formula* is then presented.

3. The *example* (and sometimes a group of several examples) shows you how to make the computation and enables you to verify that you are making it correctly yourself. Clippings from the financial press are used whenever possible.

4. The *calculator guide* provides detailed instructions for using a calculator to solve the formula.

5. How do you know you understand the computation? A *self-test* (with the answers provided) enables you to assure yourself that you can perform the calculation correctly.

You may take advantage of this format in a number of ways. Those with little or no financial background should go through each step. Those who are comfortable with the calculator may skip step 4. The advanced student might only go through step 1 (or steps 1 and 2) and step 5.

Note: All calculations may be done by hand, with pencil and paper. But using a simple calculator, while not absolutely necessary, makes things simpler, more accurate, and much quicker. Only a *simple* calculator is required—nothing elaborate or costly.

HOW TO USE THE CALCULATOR

The author used a Texas Instruments hand-held calculator, model TI-1795, for this book. It is solar-powered, requiring no batteries, only a light source. This calculator has:

- A memory function.
- A reverse-sign key.
- A combination ON/CLEAR ENTRY/CLEAR key.

While the memory function and the reverse-sign key are helpful, they are not absolutely necessary. Any simple calculator may be used.

Turning on the Calculator

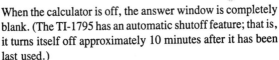

When the calculator is off, the answer window is completely blank. (The TI-1795 has an automatic shutoff feature; that is, it turns itself off approximately 10 minutes after it has been last used.)

To turn on the calculator, simply press the ON/C button (for "on/clear"). The calculator display should now show "0." [On some calculators there are separate ON/OFF, C (for "clear") and CE (for "clear entry") buttons.]

"Erasing" a Mistake

You don't have to completely clear the calculator if you make a mistake. You can clear just the last digit entered with the CE button (for "clear entry").

If you make an error while doing a calculation, you can "erase" just the last number entered rather than starting all over again.

Example: You are adding 2 and 4 but instead enter 2 plus 3. Realizing your error before you hit the equals sign, you can change the 3 to a 4.

Let's practice correcting an error. Enter 2, then +, then 3. There's the error—you entered 3 instead of 4! The calculator window now reads "3." To correct the last digit—to change from 2+3 to 2+4—press one of the following buttons *once*:

- ON/C
- C
- C/CE

Remember: Press this button only once.

Notice that the calculator window now reads "2." Pressing the ON/C button "erased" only the last number you entered, the number 3, but left everything else. The 2+ is still entered in the calculator! Now press 4, and then =. The window now reads—correctly—"6."

For such a simple calculation this seems really not worth the bother. But imagine how frustrated you would be if you were adding a very long list of figures and *then* made an error. Without the "clear entry" key, you would have to start all over again. With it, you can simply erase the last digit entered (the wrong number) and replace it with the correct number.

Clearing the Calculator

Clearing a calculator is similar to erasing a blackboard: All previous entries are erased, or "cleared." Each calculation should be performed on a "cleared" calculator, just as you must, for example, write on a clean blackboard.

You know the calculator is cleared when the answer window shows "0." Most calculators are cleared when they are turned on.

If *anything* other than "0." shows, the calculator is not cleared. You must press one of the following buttons twice, depending on how your calculator is equipped:

- ON/C
- C
- C/CE

(With the TI-1795, anything showing in the window may be cleared by pressing the ON/C button *twice*. With this model, when digits appear in the window, pressing the ON/C button once clears only the last digit entered.)

This erases everything you have entered into the calculator. When you begin the next computation, it will be with a "clean slate."

Some calculators have separate CE (clear entry) and C (clear calculator) buttons. (The TI-1795 combines them into the "on" button. When the window is blank, pressing it once turns the calculator on. When any numbers show in the window, pressing it once erases the last number entered (clear entry); pressing it twice erases all previous entries.)

Example: Let's return to the previous example. Enter 2, then +, then 3. The window shows "3.," the last number entered. Now press the ON/C button. The window now shows "2." At this point you have erased the last number entered (clear entry). Now press the ON/C button a second time. The window now reads "0." The calculator is completely cleared.

Clearing Memory

Calculators with a memory function have several buttons labeled "M+" and "Mr/C." When the memory function is in use, the letter "M" appears in the calculator window. To clear the memory, press the Mr/C button *twice*. This should eliminate the M from the display. If any numbers remain, they can be cleared by pressing the ON/C button, once or twice, until the calculator reads "0."

Calculator Guides

Almost all the formulas described in this text include very specific calculator instructions, or Calculator Guides. You should be able to "skip" these instructions after you have done a number of calculations successfully, but they will be there should you need them.

These Calculator Guides are complete; they show you exactly which buttons to press, and in what sequence, to arrive at the correct answer. Each Calculator Guide section starts with an arrowhead (▶), which indicates that you should clear your calculator. When you see this symbol, be sure that the calculator window shows only "0." No other digits, nor the letter M, should appear.

Following the arrowhead symbol are the buttons to press. Press *only* the buttons indicated.

The second arrowhead (◀) indicates that the calculation is completed and that the numbers following it, always in bold, show the correct answer. The figures in bold will be exactly the numbers that will appear in your calculator's window!

Example: Multiply 2.564 and 85.953.

CALCULATOR GUIDE

▶ 2.564 × 85.953 = ◀ **220.38349**

Try it! Follow the instructions in the line above on your calculator.

- Clear the calculator.
- Enter the numbers, decimal points, and arithmetic signs, exactly as indicated: 2.564 × 85.953.
- Your calculator display should read "220.38349."

Let's try something a little more complicated.

Example:

$$\blacktriangleright \quad \frac{45.98}{346} \times \frac{197.45}{93.4} = ?$$

The problem may be solved long-hand by first multiplying the two top numbers, and then dividing the resulting figure first by one bottom number and then by the other bottom number. There are a few other methods as well, but let's see how fast and simple it is by using the calculator. Here are the instructions:

CALCULATOR GUIDE

▶ 45.98 × 197.45 ÷ 346 ÷ 93.4 = ◀ **0.2809332**

If you didn't arrive at that answer, redo the calculation precisely according to the Calculator Guide instructions. If you enter the figures correctly, it will work!

SELF-TEST

Perform the following calculations. *Write* your answers down, and then check them against the correct answers given at the end of this section.

A. 0.945 ÷ 56.96

B. 854 × 65.99

C. 56.754 × 92.532 ÷ 5229

D. 23 − 6.5 × 88

E. 54.9 + 23.458 × 95 ÷ 64.11

ANSWERS TO SELF-TEST

A. 0.0165905

B. 56355.46

C. 1.0043146

D. 1452.

E. 116.11308

If you did the problems correctly, even though not until the second or third try, you will have no trouble doing any of the calculations in this book.

Rounding Off

Most Wall Street calculations require that you show only two digits to the right of the decimal place—for example, 98.74 rather than 98.74285.

To round off to two decimal places, you must examine the *third* digit to the right of the decimal.

- If the third digit is less than 5 (4, 3, 2, 1, or 0), then ignore all digits after the second one to the right of the decimal.

Example: In the number 98.74285, the third digit after the decimal point is 2 (less than 5). You reduce the number to 98.74

- If the third digit after the decimal is 5 or more (5, 6, 7, 8, or 9), increase the second digit after the decimal by one.

Example: In the number 67.12863, the third digit after the decimal is 8 (5 or more). So you increase the second post-decimal digit by one, changing the second digit, 2, to a 3! The rounded number becomes 67.13.

Not all computations require two digits after the decimal. Whatever the requirement, the rounding off process is basically the same. For instance, to round off to a whole number, examine the *first* digit after the decimal.

● If it is 4 or less, ignore all the digits after the decimal point.

Example: To round 287.382 to a whole number, examine the first digit after the decimal (3). Since it is 4 or less, reduce the number to 287.

● If the first digit after the decimal is 5 or greater, increase the number immediately before the decimal by 1.

Example: Round off 928.519. Because the first digit after the decimal is 5 (more than 4), you add 1 to the number just before the decimal place: 928.519 is rounded off to 929.

Some numbers seem to jump greatly in value when rounded upward.

Example: Round 39.6281 to a whole number. It becomes 40! Round 2699.51179 to a whole number. It becomes 2700!

SELF-TEST

Make certain that you follow the correct process in rounding the following numbers to two decimal places:

A. 1.18283

B. 1.1858

C. 27.333

D. 27.3392

E. 817.391

F. 7289.99499

ANSWERS TO SELF-TEST

A. 1.18

B. 1.19

C. 27.33

D. 27.34

E. 817.39

F. 7289.99

"Chain" Calculations

A useful time-saver when using the calculator is chain multiplication and division. It comes into play when you have to:

- Multiply a given number by several other numbers.
- Divide several numbers by the same number.

Example: You have a series of multiplication problems with a single multiplier.

    31.264 × 0.095   31.264 × 2.73   31.264 × 95.1

To solve all these calculations, you can enter the figure 31.264 once. It is not necessary to clear the calculator between problems.

CALCULATOR GUIDE

▶   31.264 × 0.095 = ◀ **2.97008**
     2.73 ×   = ◀ **85.35072**
     95.1 ×   = ◀ **2973.2064**

Here's how this "chain" of multiplications is done.

- Enter the first problem (31.264 × 0.095). The answer is 2.97008.
- Enter 2.73 (the next multiplicand) and press the equals key (=). The answer for the next multiplication (85.35072) appears in the window.
- Enter 95.1 and equals (=), and the third answer is displayed (2973.2064).

If you had to repeat the common multiplicand for all three operations, you would have to press keys 38 times. This feature reduces that number to just 22—a real time-saver that also decreases the chances of error.

Example: Let's see how "chain" division works.

▶   31.58 ÷ 3.915   4769.773 ÷ 3.915   .63221 ÷ 3.915

You can solve all three problems by entering the figure 3.915 and the division sign ($\div$) only once.

▶ 31.58 $\div$ 3.915 = ◀ **8.0664112**
  4769.773 $\div$ = ◀ **1218.3328**
  0.63221 $\div$ = ◀ **0.161484**

- Enter the first problem (31.58 $\div$ 3.915). The answer is 8.0664112.

- Enter only 4769.773 (the next dividend) and the equals sign (=). The second answer (1218.3328) appears in the window.

- Then enter 0.63221 and press the equals key, to get the third answer (0.161484).

Some 42 keystrokes are thus reduced to 28.

CONTENTS

THE NYIF
VEST-POCKET GUIDE TO
STOCK BROKERAGE MATH

CHAPTER 1

PRICING STOCKS

Dollars and Eighths

Stocks are traditionally priced (quoted) in dollars and eighths of dollars.

Example: A stock trading (in dollars and cents) at $24.25 is quoted as 24¼. While 24¼ is, of course, equal to 24.25, the Wall Street tradition persists. Note also that stock prices are not preceded by a dollar sign ($); it is simply understood that the price is in dollars.

Also, stock price changes are measured in eighths of dollars. A stock quoted at 45½ per share is selling for 45 and one-half dollars—which equals $45.50. The next higher price is 45⅝ ($45.625), and the next higher price after that is 45¾ ($45.75).

Example: Here's an entire price sequence from 16 ($16.00) to 17 ($17.00):

16

16⅛

16¼

16⅜

16½

16⅝

16¾

16⅞

17

An eighth of a dollar is 12½ cents ($0.125), a quarter dollar is 25 cents ($0.25), three-eighths is 37½ cents ($0.375), and so on. Since memorizing these figures is a lot easier than figuring them out each time, why not learn them now! We will show you how to use the calculator to compute them, but your financial calculations will be a lot easier if you study the chart until you have them down pat. (Think how difficult simple arithmetic would be if you didn't know your multiplication tables!)

Fraction	Dollar Equivalent
1/8	$0.125
1/4	$0.25
3/8	$0.375
1/2	$0.50
5/8	$0.625
3/4	$0.75
7/8	$0.875

Note that each fraction is 1/8 higher than the previous fraction—higher by 12½ cents!

Some of these fractions require no computation. Anyone can see that a 1/4 is 25 cents, a half is 50 cents, and 3/4 is 75 cents. The "tougher" ones (1/8, 3/8, 5/8, and 7/8) are not so tough; they require only a simple calculation. The formula for converting these fractions to dollars and cents is simple: Divide the numerator (top number of the fraction) by the denominator (8). (Keep the answer to three decimal places.)

CALCULATOR GUIDE
Examples: To find the dollar equivalent of 1/8, divide the numerator (1) by the denominator (8):

▶ 1 ÷ 8 = ◀ **0.125**   (12½ cents)

To find the dollar equivalent of 3/8:

▶ 3 ÷ 8 = ◀ **0.375**   (37½ cents)

To find the dollar equivalent of 5/8:

▶ 5 ÷ 8 = ◀ **0.625**   (62½ cents)

To find the dollar equivalent of 7/8·

▶ 7 ÷ 8 = ◀ **0.875**   (87½ cents)

Let's convert a few stock prices into dollars and cents. Note that, in the following conversions, the dollar amounts are carried over as is. You arrive at the cents amounts either by adding the memorized values to the dollar amounts or by means of the preceding calculation.

Stock Price Listing	Dollars and Cents
24	$ 24.00
36½	$ 36.50
8⅛	$ 8.125
109⅞	$109.875
55¾	$ 55.75
4⅝	$ 4.625
144	$144.00
21¼	$ 21.25
73⅜	$ 73.375

Round Lots, Odd Lots

Each quotation in this table shows the value of a single share at the listed price. While it is possible to purchase just one share of stock, most people buy stocks in lots of 100 shares, or in a multiple of 100 shares, such as 300, 800, 2,300, or 8,600. These multiples are called *round lots*. Amounts of stock from 1 to 99 shares are called *odd lots*. A 200-share block of stock is a round lot; 58 shares is an odd lot.

To value a given stock holding, multiply the number of shares held by the per-share price.

Dollar value = Number of shares × Per-share price

Example: XYZ stock is selling at 36½ per share. 100 shares of XYZ would be worth $3,650.00:

100 shares × 36.50 = 3,650.00

200 shares (2 round lots) of ABC at 129¾ per share would be worth $25,950.00.

200 shares × 129.75 = 25,950.00

Example: What is the current value of 250 shares of CDE selling at 37¼ per share?

250 × 37.25 = $9,312.50

CALCULATOR GUIDE

▶ 250 × 37.25 = ◀ **9312.5**

This is $9,312.50!

Note: The calculator did not show the final zero; *you* have to add it.

SELF-TEST I

What is the dollar value of the following stock positions?

A. 100 shares @ 23¼

B. 250 shares @ 5⅜

C. 2,500 shares @ 34⅝

D. 35 shares @ 109

E. What is the total dollar value of *all* the preceding positions?

SELF-TEST II

Figure 1-1 from the financial press shows a number of stock price listings. If your client owns 100 shares of *each* of the first three issues listed, what would be the *total* value of her holdings? Use the *closing* prices for each security.

Figure 1-1
New York Stock Exchange Composite Transactions

52 Weeks Hi	Lo	Stock	Sym	Div	Yld %	PE	Vol 100s	Hi	Lo	Close	Net Chg
29¼	22¼	Minn P&L	MPL	1.90	6.7	14	182	28½	28¼	28⅜	− ⅛
31¼	12¾	MirageResrt	MIR	...	...	26	1063	25⅛	24⅝	25	+ ⅜
2⅛	¹³⁄₁₆	Mitel	MLT	...	...	...	77	1⅛	1	1⅛	+ ⅛
20⅝	11⅜	MitsubBk	MBK	.06e	.3	...	5	19¾	19¾	19¾	− ⅛
69¾	55⅛	Mobil Cp	MOB	3.20	4.8	13	4352	68	66½	66⅝	− ¼
27¼	13⅛	MolclrBio	MB	...	...	...	267	26½	26⅛	26⅜	...
14	8¾	MonarchM	MMO	.20	2.1	...	18	9¾	9½	9¾	+ ¼
76	38¾	Monsanto	MTC	2.08	2.8	43	4389	75⅞	74¼	74¾	− ¾
23¼	17⅜	MontPwr	MTP	1.48	6.4	12	406	23¼	23	23¼	+ ⅜
14⅞	10	Montedisn	MNT	.38e	3.7	...	14	10⅝	10⅜	10⅜	− ¼
20¼	15	MontgSt	MTS	1.76	8.9	...	45	19¾	19⅜	19¾	+ ⅜
28½	21	Moore Cp	MCL	.94	3.7	22	546	25¾	25¼	25¾	+ ⅜
12½	7¼	MorganGren	MGC	.90e	9.5	...	100	10⅝	10⅜	...	...

(Courtesy of *The Wall Street Journal,* August 26, 1991.)

ANSWERS TO SELF-TEST I

A. $ 2,325.00 (100 × 23.25)

B. $ 1,343.75 (250 × 5.375)

C. $86,562.50 (2500 × 34.625)

D. $ 3,815.00 (35 × 109)

E. $94,046.25 (Add the first four answers.)

ANSWER TO SELF-TEST II

$5,450.00
(100 × 28.375) + (100 × 25) + (100 × 1.125)
   2837.50   +   2500.   +   112.50   = 5450.

CHAPTER 2

PRICING CORPORATE BONDS

Bond Quotations

Bonds issued by corporations (as opposed to bonds issued by municipalities and the federal government) trade in points and eighths *as a percent of par*.

One bond is considered to have a par value of $1,000. This means that, if you own one bond, the company issuing the bond will pay you $1,000 when the bond matures. This $1,000 is the bond's *par* value, also called its *face* value. Either term means the amount of the loan represented by the bond, that is, the amount the issuing company has borrowed and must repay when the due date (*maturity date*) arrives.

It is extremely unlikely that an investor will own just one bond. In fact, it is very rare that bonds are even issued in "pieces" as small as a single bond with a total par value of only $1,000. A corporate bond "round lot" is considered to be *10* bonds, and it is very difficult to find even 5-bond lots. The notation for one bond is 1M. This means 1 bond of $1,000 par—a total par value of $1,000. Traders and investors call this "one bond," and they would write an order for this bond as "1 M."

A bond with a total par value of $10,000 is written as "10 M," and the lot would be referred to as "ten bonds." A bond with a total par value of $100,000 would be called "100 bonds," written out as "100 M." A quarter-million dollars worth of bonds would be called "250 bonds" and would be written as "250 M."

Even though single bonds (1 M) aren't common, we will use one bond with a total par value of $1,000 in many of our examples for the sake of simplicity. If you are dealing with a 25-bond block, it is a simple matter to treat it as one bond and then to multiply your result by 25 at the end of the calculation.

Bond prices look like stock prices, but there is a big difference: Stock prices are in dollars and eighths of dollars, while bond prices are expressed as a percent of par value.

Example: When a bond is quoted at 98, it is selling *not* for $98, but 98 *percent* (%) of its par value. Since each bond has a par value of $1,000, one bond trading at 98 is worth 98% of its $1,000 par value.

$$0.98 \ (98\%) \times \$1,000 = \$980$$

If a stock is trading at 98, it is worth $98 per share. A corporate bond selling at 98 is worth $980!

There are several mathematical methods for converting bond quotes to dollar values. Each of the following methods may be used to convert 1 bond's (1M) quoted price into dollars and cents. Use whichever of the following methods works best for you. Each method is demonstrated by example.

Example: Find the dollar value of a bond quoted at 96½.

- Convert the fraction in the price to a decimal, divide by 100, and then multiply by $1,000.

$$\frac{96\frac{1}{2}}{100} \times \$1,000 = \frac{96.5}{100} \times \$1,000 = \frac{\$96,500}{100} = \$965.$$

- Convert the fraction in the price to a decimal in your head, move the decimal place two digits to the left, and then multiply by $1,000.

$$96\frac{1}{2} = 96.5, \text{ then } 0.965$$
$$0.965 \times \$1,000 = \$965.$$

- Convert the fraction in the price to a decimal in your head, and then multiply by ten.

$$96\tfrac{1}{2} = 96.5$$
$$96.5 \times 10 = \$965$$

- Convert the fraction in the price to a decimal in your head, and then move the decimal one place to the right.

$$96\tfrac{1}{2} = 96.5$$
$$96.5 \text{ becomes } 965. \text{ or } \$965.$$

The author finds it easiest to use the last method. You simply treat the bond price as a stock price and convert the fraction to a decimal (1/2 becomes 0.5, 3/4 becomes .75, etc.). Then multiply by 10 by moving the decimal point one place to the right.

Any of these methods gives the dollar value for *one* bond at that price. If you are dealing wth more than one bond, multiply again by the number of bonds involved. (Did you memorize the fraction conversion table in Chapter 1? It will make your bond calculations much easier as well.)

Let's try this easy method for several different bond prices.

Example: What is the dollar value of one bond (1M) selling at 88⅜?

- First convert 88⅜ to its decimal equivalent, 88.375.
- Multiply by 10, which gives 883.75 or $883.75.

Reminder: You can "multiply by 10" simply by moving the decimal one place to the right. In this instance, 88.375 changes to 883.75

CALCULATOR GUIDE

▶ 3 ÷ 8 = ◀ **0.375**

Then

▶ 88.375 × 10 = ◀ **883.75** or $883.75

Note that you can skip a whole step if you have the decimal

equivalents for eighths memorized! If you know that 3/8 equals 0.375, you multiply 88.375 by ten (or move the decimal one place to the right) to find the dollar value for a single bond.

Example: What is the dollar value of 25 bonds (25M) trading at 102¾?

- Since the fraction involved is an "easy" one, 102¾ becomes 102.75.

- Multiply 102.75 by 10 to get the dollar value of one bond: $1,027.50.

- Multiplying again by 25 gives the dollar value for 25 bonds: $25,687.50

CALCULATOR GUIDE

▶ 3 ÷ 4 = ▶ 0.75

Then

▶ 102.75 × 10 × 25 = ▶ **25687.5** or **$25,687.50**

Premium, Par, and Discount

Bonds may trade at a discount, at par, or at a premium.

- *Discount bonds are valued at less than $1,000:* Bond prices that are less than 100, such as 94¼, 97, and 98⅜, are said to be *discount* prices. When a discount price is converted to dollars, the answer is always less than $1,000! Therefore, if a $1,000 par bond is trading at less than 100% of its face value, it must be selling for less than $1,000.

- *Par bonds are worth exactly $1,000:* Bonds occasionally trade exactly at 100, that is, at 100% of their $1,000 par value, which is of course exactly $1,000. Such bonds are *said to be trading at par.*

- *Premium bonds have a value greater than $1,000:* When bonds are priced above 100—such as 100⅞, 102 or 158¼—they are said to be trading at a *premium.* Premium bonds are valued at more than $1,000 per bond.

Figure 2-1
Corporate Bond Quotations

CORPORATION BONDS
Volume, $39,580,018

Bonds	Cur Yld	Vol	Close		Net Chg.
AForP 5s30	9.9	26	50½	−	½
AMR 9s16	9.5	10	94⅜	+	1⅞
AMR zr06	...	59	41¼	+	⅝
Advst 9s08	cv	56	76⅞	+	1⅞
AetnLf 8⅛07	8.6	33	95	+	¾
AlaP 8¼s03	8.4	5	98½	+	2¾
AlaP 9¾s04	9.5	17	102⅞	−	1⅛
AlaP 9½08	9.3	13	102½	−	½
AlskAr zr06	...	5	32½	−	1
AlldC zr98	...	8	55	+	1
AlldC zr92	...	90	93	+	½
AlldC zr96	...	20	70	−	¾
AlldC zr2000	...	15	45¼	−	⅛
AlldC zr95	...	10	73	−	¼
AlldC zr97	...	5	59	−	½
AlldC zr03	...	40	33¼	−	½
AlldC zr09	...	105	18¾	+	¼
AlskH 11⅜93	11.2	1	101¼	−	¼
AMAX 14½94	12.6	47	115½	−	⅜
[illegible]	[illegible]	[illegible]	[illegible]		

(Courtesy of *The Wall Street Journal*, August 26, 1991.)

SELF-TEST

See Figure 2-1.

A. What is the dollar value of 10 M AMR 9s16 bonds?

B. What is the dollar value of 100 M AMR zr06 bonds?

C. Are any of the first 5 bonds listed selling at a premium?

ANSWERS TO SELF-TEST

A. $9,437.50 (94.375 × 10 × 10)

B. $41,250.00 (41.25 × 10 × 100)

C. No. They are all trading at discount prices of less than 100 (less than $1,000 per bond).

CHAPTER 3

PRICING GOVERNMENT BONDS AND NOTES

Treasury Bond and Note Quotations

Among the debt instruments issued by the U.S. government are:

- Treasury notes, with maturities of up to 10 years.
- Treasury bonds, maturities of more than 10 years.

Like corporate bonds, Treasury notes and bonds are quoted as a percentage of their par value (see Chapter 2). The unit of trading for governments, however, is much smaller than it is for corporates. Treasury bonds and notes are traded in points and thirty-seconds (32nds) of points, rather than in points and eighths (8ths) of points.

Why is that? *Governments*, as they are called, normally trade in much larger blocks than corporates—a round lot is $1,000,000! So a one-eighth spread between the bid and asked prices for a block of $10,000 corporate bonds (10M) amounts to $12.50. A one-eighth spread on a $1,000,000 worth of government bonds (1MM) is $1,250! That's too big a difference for trading purposes, and so governments are traded in 32nds to give traders more flexibility in negotiating prices.

There's one other small difference. Whereas corporate bond prices make use of fractions (such as 96¼), government prices make use of a colon to separate the whole number from the fractional part.

Example: The price for a government bond is 99:08. This means that the bond is trading for 99⁸/₃₂% of its par value. That's correct, 99⁸/₃₂%! The number following the decimal (8) is the numerator for the fraction: 99:8 = 99⁸/₃₂%.

Treasury Bond and Note Prices

Treasury bonds and notes have face (or par) values of $1,000 (like corporate bonds). Government price computations are a little trickier than pricing corporate bonds, but the general principle is the same:

- Reduce any fraction to its decimal equivalent. To reduce the fraction to its decimal equivalent, simply divide the fraction's numerator (the top number) by its denominator (the bottom number).
- Move the decimal point one place to the right to get the dollar value of one bond.

Example: What is the price of a "T-bond" quoted at 99:08?

- Reduce the fraction to its decimal equivalent. Divide the fraction's numerator (the top number, 8) by its denominator (the bottom number, 32).

$$99:08 = 99⁸/₃₂ = 99.25$$

- Move the decimal point one place to the right to get the dollar value of one bond.

$$99.25 = \$992.50 \text{ per bond}$$

CALCULATOR GUIDE

▶ 8 ÷ 32 = ◀ 0.25

Note: A *corporate* bond worth $992.50 would be quoted as "99¼," while a *government* bond worth that same dollar amount would be quoted as "99:08." It is important to remember this difference between corporate and government quotations: For "T-bond" or "T-note" quotations, everything to the right of the colon represents 32nds!

Examples:

Corporate Bond Bond Quote	Government Bond Quote	Dollar Value for One Bond
97⅛	97:04	$ 971.25
102¼	102:08	$1,022.50
98⅜	98:12	$ 983.75
110½	110:16	$1,105.00
96⅝	96:20	$ 966.25
100¾	100:24	$1,007.50
99⅞	99:28	$ 998.75

See Figure 3-1 for the full range of government bond and note fractions. Any of the fractions can quite easily be reduced to decimal equivalents by dividing the number of 32nds (the number after the colon) by 32.

Example: To figure out the dollar value of :17 (17/32), divide 17 by 32: $17 \div 32 = 0.53125$.

- Multiply 0.53125 by the face value of the government ($1,000): $0.53125 \times \$1,000 = \$5.3125$.
- Or move the decimal one place to the right: 0.53125 becomes 5.3125, or $5.3125.

CALCULATOR GUIDE

▶ $17 \div 32 \times 10 =$ ◀ **5.3125**   That's $5.3125 per bond.

To calculate the price of a government bond or note, given the quote:

- Reduce the quoted price to its decimal equivalent.
- Move the decimal one place to the right, which has the same effect as multiplying the decimal equivalent by 10—thus giving the value for a single bond.

Examples: What is the dollar value of a government bond (1M) trading at 99:16?

- Reduce the quoted price to its decimal equivalent.

$$99:16 = 99^{16}\!/_{32} = 99.5$$

Figure 3-1
Government Bond/Note Quotations

Price	Fraction	Decimal Equivalent	Dollar Value per Bond
:01	1/32	.03125	$0.3125
:02	2/32	.0625	$0.625
:03	3/32	.09375	$0.9375
:04	4/32	.125	$1.25
:05	5/32	.15625	$1.5625
:06	6/32	.1875	$1.875
:07	7/32	.21875	$2.1875
:08	8/32	.25	$2.50
:09	9/32	.28125	$2.8125
:10	10/32	.3125	$3.125
:11	11/32	.34375	$3.4375
:12	12/32	.375	$3.75
:13	13/32	.40625	$4.0625
:14	14/32	.4375	$4.375
:15	15/32	.46875	$4.6875
:16	16/32	.50	$5.00
:17	17/32	.53125	$5.3125
:18	18/32	.5625	$5.625
:19	19/32	.59375	$5.9375
:20	20/32	.625	$6.25
:21	21/32	.65625	$6.5625
:22	22/32	.6875	$6.875
:23	23/32	.71875	$7.1875
:24	24/32	.75	$7.50
:25	25/32	.78125	$7.8125
:26	26/32	.8125	$8.125
:27	27/32	.84375	$8.4375
:28	28/32	.875	$8.75
:29	29/32	.90625	$9.0625
:30	30/32	.9375	$9.375
:31	31/32	.96875	$9.6875

● Move the decimal one place to the right.

$$99.5 = 995. = \$995.00$$

The price of one bond is $995.00.

CALCULATOR GUIDE

▶ 16 ÷ 32 = ◀ **0.5**

▶ 99.5 × 10 = ◀ **995.** or **$995.00**

Note: Multiplying by 10 (as you just did in the Calculator Guide) is the same as moving the decimal one place to the right. Multiplying by 100 moves the decimal point 2 places, multiplying by 1,000 moves the decimal 3 places, and so on. The decimal moves one place for each zero.

Example: What is the dollar value of 100M par value of government bonds trading at 102:08?

$$102{:}08 = 102^{8/32} = 102.25$$
$$102.25 \times 10 = \$1,022.50$$

The value of *one* bond is $1,022.50.

$$\$1,022.50 \times 100 \text{ bonds} = \$102,250$$

This is the value of *100* bonds.

Note: You can perform the same calculation by:

- First moving the decimal one place to the right (thus multiplying by 10), which gives the one-bond value.
- Then moving the decimal two more places to the right, which gives the value for 100 bonds.

CALCULATOR GUIDE

▶ 8 ÷ 32 = ◀ **0.25**

Then

▶ 102.25 × 10 × 100 = ◀ **102250.** or $102,250.

Note: You can skip the first step (dividing 8 by 32) if you realize that 8/32 is equal to 1/4 (see Figure 2-2): 1/4 becomes 0.25. You can then multiply 102.25 (102:08) first by 10 to get the one-bond value and then by 100 to get the 100-bond value!

Chain Calculations

Sometimes it is necessary to reduce a series of government prices to dollar-and-cent amounts. This is when "chain," or consecutive, calculations come into play. Most calculators are capable of doing "chain" calculations, thereby saving the user a lot of time. In the case of governments, you would need to divide numerators by the common denominator (32).

Note: In chain calculations, do *not* clear the calculator after the first computation. Nor is it necessary to reenter the divide sign, the multiply sign, or the common figure in the chain. Your calculator can also do chain mutiplication! [See "How to Use the Calculator" ("Chain Calculations") at the front of the book.]

Example: You are reducing several government bond fractions, such as 9/32, 11/32, 13/32 and 15/32, to decimal equivalents.

- Divide 9 by 32. After you press the equals button (=), the calculator will show 0.28125, which is the answer.
- Without clearing the calculator, enter 11 and then = . The calculator will now read 0.34375, the answer to 11/32. [Note that you did not have to reenter the division sign (÷) or the common figure (32).]
- Again, without clearing the calculator, enter 13 and then = . The calculator now shows 0.40625, the answer to 13/32.
- Now press 15 and then = , and the calculator will read 0.46875, the answer to 15/32.

CALCULATOR GUIDE
In chain calculations, you must "catch" the answer (the figures in parentheses) before entering the next numerator.

▶ 9 ÷ 32 = (0.28125) 11 = (0.34375) 13 = (0.40625) 15
= ◀ 0.46875

Note: You did not have to reenter the division sign (÷) or the common figure (32).

SELF-TEST
Use Figure 3-2 to answer the following. Use the *asked* prices in each instance.

A. What is the dollar value of 10M 8⅝ Aug 97n notes?

B. What is the dollar value of 100M 11⅝ Jan 92n notes?

C. What is the dollar value of 1MM ($1,000,000) 3½ Nov98 bonds?

Figure 3-2
Treasury Bond and Note Quotations

Monday, August 26, 1991

Representative Over-the-Counter quotations based on transactions of $1 million or more.

Treasury bond, note and bill quotes are as of mid-afternoon. Colons in bid-and-asked quotes represent 32nds; 101:01 means 101 1/32. Net changes in 32nds. n-Treasury note. Treasury bill quotes in hundredths, quoted on terms of a rate of discount. Days to maturity calculated from settlement date. All yields are to maturity and based on the asked quote. For bonds callable prior to maturity, yields are computed to the earliest call date for issues quoted above par and to the maturity date for issues below par. *-When issued.
Source: Federal Reserve Bank of New York.

U.S. Treasury strips as of 3 p.m. Eastern time, also based on transactions of $1 million or more. Colons in bid-and-asked quotes represent 32nds; 101:01 means 101 1/32. Net changes in 32nds. Yields calculated on the bid quotation. ci-stripped coupon interest. bp-Treasury bond, stripped principal. np-Treasury note, stripped principal. For bonds callable prior to maturity, yields are computed to the earliest call date for issues quoted above par and to the maturity date for issues below par.
Source: Bear, Stearns & Co. via Street Software Technology Inc.

GOVT. BONDS & NOTES					Ask	Rate	Maturity Mo/Yr	Bid	Asked	Chg.	Ask
Rate	Maturity	Bid	Asked	Chg.	Yld.						Yld.
8¼	Aug 91n	100:00	100:02	....	0.56	8½	Jul 97n	104:03	104:05	− 8	7.61
8⅜	Sep 91n	100:08	100:10	− 1	4.73	8⅝	Aug 97n	104:23	104:25	− 9	7.61
9⅛	Sep 91n	100:11	100:13	....	4.44	8¾	Oct 97n	105:09	105:11	− 8	7.64
12¼	Oct 91n	100:27	100:29	− 2	5.07	8⅞	Nov 97n	105:27	105:29	− 7	7.66
7⅝	Oct 91n	100:10	100:12	− 1	5.32	7⅞	Jan 98n	100:28	100:30	− 8	7.69
6½	Nov 91n	100:05	100:07	....	5.37	8⅛	Feb 98n	102:05	102:07	− 9	7.68
8½	Nov 91n	100:18	100:20	− 1	5.4⅛	7⅞	Apr 98n	100:23	100:25	− 9	7.72
14¼	Nov 91n	101:26	101:28	− 2	5.21	7	May 93-98	96:01	96:09	− 9	7.72
7¾	Nov 91n	100:16	100:18	− 1	5.43	9	May 98n	106:15	106:17	− 8	7.74
7⅝	Dec 91n	100:20	100:22	− 1	5.50	8¼	Jul 98n	102:21	102:23	− 8	7.73
8¼	Dec 91n	100:27	100:29	− 1	5.46	9¼	Aug 98n	107:26	107:28	− 8	7.76
11⅝	Jan 92n	102:06	102:08	− 2	5.51	3½	Nov 98	94:07	95:07	− 5	4.28
8⅛	Jan 92n	100:31	101:01	− 2	5.60	8⅞	Nov 98n	105:26	105:28	− 9	7.80
6⅝	Feb 92n	100:11	100:13	− 1	5.71	8⅞	Feb 99n	105:26	105:28	− 9	7.82
9⅛	Feb 92n	101:15	101:17	− 1	5.72	8½	May 94-99	102:02	102:10	− 4	7.54
14⅝	Feb 92n	104:01	104:03	− 3	5.56	9⅛	May 99n	107:06	107:08	−10	7.85
8½	Feb 92n	101:10	101:12	− 3	5.72	8	Aug 99n	100:29	100:31	− 7	7.83
7⅞	Mar 92n	101:06	101:08	− 2	5.69	7⅞	Nov 99n	100:01	100:03	− 7	7.86
8½	Mar 92n	101:17	101:19	− 2	5.72	7⅞	Feb 95-00	99:26	99:30	− 3	7.89
11¾	Apr 92n	103:21	103:23	− 2	5.68	8½	Feb 00n	103:20	103:22	− 7	7.89
8⅞	Apr 92n	101:31	102:01	− 2	5.77	8⅞	May 00n	105:25	105:27	− 9	7.93
						8⅜	Aug 95-00	101:27	101:31	− 4	7.79

(Courtesy of *The Wall Street Journal,* August 27, 1991.)

ANSWERS TO SELF-TEST

A. $10,478.125 (104.78125 × 10 × 10)

B. $102,250. (102.25 × 10 × 100)

C. $952,187.50 (95.21875 × 10 × 1000)

CHAPTER 4

DIVIDEND PAYMENTS

All financially "healthy" preferred stocks, and many common stocks, pay dividends. These are usually cash payments. On occasion, corporations will pay *stock* dividends, instead of cash dividends to their common shareholders, and some corporations pay common stockholders *both* cash and stock dividends!

A company's dividend policy—that is, the timing and amount of any dividends paid—is set by the board of directors. Most dividend-paying companies make cash distributions on a quarterly basis, paying dividends four times a year. This is not a legal requirement, and some companies pay out on other schedules, but it definitely is the norm.

Ex-Dividend and Cum-Dividend Dates

To receive a forthcoming cash dividend, you must purchase the underlying stock, regular way, *before* the ex-dividend date. Those buying the stock *on or after* the ex-date will not receive the dividend.

The Wall Street Journal prints a "Corporate Dividend News" column each business day. It lists the dividends declared by various corporate boards of directors the *previous* day, as well as the stocks that will sell ex-dividend the *following* business day. The column is shown in Figure 4-1.

Example: The "Dividend News" in Figure 4-1 appeared on August 27th, listing the stocks selling ex-dividend the following day, August 28. Anyone wishing to purchase these stocks *and* receive the dividend must buy the same day as the article appeared, August 27th.

Figure 4-1
Corporate Dividend News

Dividends Reported August 26

Company	Period	Amt.	Payable date	Record date
REGULAR				
Ameriana Bancorp	Q	.14	10- 4-91	9-20
CNB Bancshares	Q	.22	10- 1-91	9-20
Crane Co	Q	.18¾	9-13-91	9- 6
Ingles Markets clA	Q	.05½	10-15-91	9-30
PHH Corp	Q	.30	10-31-91	10-11
Provena Foods Inc	Q	.03½	9-30-91	9-10
Raymond James Finl	Q	.06	10- 7-91	9-16
Sizzler Intl Inc	Q	.04	10-11-91	9-25
Standard Products	Q	.12	10-22-91	10- 8
Yankee Energy Sys	Q	.40	9-27-91	9- 6
FUNDS · REITS · INVESTMENT COS · LPS				
Bull&Bear Hi Yld	M	.06	8-30-91	8-26
NatlSecsCalTxExmpt	M	h.072	8-26-91	8-26
NatlMultiSec Fixed	M	h.10½	8-26-91	8-26
NatlSecsTxExmpt Bd	M	h.059	8-26-91	8-26
Property Cap Tr	Q	.10	9-16-91	9- 4
STOCK				
North Coast Energy		n	9-24-91	9-10
n-Two-for-one stock split.				
FOREIGN				
DeBeers ConslMines	—	t.242	11-22-91	9-27
GoldFlds Prop SA	—	t.059	10- 9-91	8-30
Westpac Bkg pf ADR	—	t.75	10-10-91	9- 9
INITIAL				
Medusa Corp	—	.10	9-13-91	9- 6

A-Annual; b-Payable in Canadian funds; h-From income; k-From capital gains; M-Monthly; Q-Quarterly; S-Semi-annual; t-Approximate U.S. dollar amount per American Depositary Receipt/Share.

* * *

Stocks Ex-Dividend August 28

Company	Amount	Company	Amount
Anthony Indus	.11	Kansas Pwr&Lt	.46½
Avery Dennison Cp	.20	McDonald's Corp	.09¼
Avon Products	3.00	Morgan Stanley Grp	n
Beneficial Corp	.65	n-Two-for-one stock split.	
Beneficial $4.30pf	2.15		
Continental Corp	.65	PaineWebber Group	.13
Dole Food Co Inc	.10	PaineWeb $1.375pf	.34⅜
First Bank System	.20½	Property Cap Tr	.10
Halliburton Co	.25	Union Camp Corp	.39
Home Depot Inc	.03	Union Electric Co	.54

(Courtesy of *The Wall Street Journal,* August 27, 1991.)

If you "miss" the pre-ex-dividend date deadline and do not receive the dividend, you don't necessarily suffer an economic loss. In theory, the stock will sell at a lower price on and just after the ex-dividend date to reflect the fact that the dividend is no longer "attached" to any stock now purchased. All other things being equal, the stock should sell lower by about the amount of the missing dividend.

Example: If a stock is trading at 88 ($88 per share) and then goes "ex" for a $1 per share dividend, the stock will most probably trade at 87 on the ex date. This, of course, presupposes that no other market forces are at play, such as a general rise or fall in the market or unusual buying or selling in that stock. In this instance the stock will sell at 88 *with* the $1 dividend (*cum* dividend), and at 87 *without* the dividend (*ex*-dividend).

Computing the Dollar Value of a Dividend

Holders are entitled to receive the stated rate for each share they own. To determine the total amount of the dividend to be received, multiply the per-share amount of the dividend by the number of shares held.

Example: An owner of 100 shares of a stock paying a per-share dividend of $1 will recive a total of $100 (100 shares × $1 per-share dividend); an owner of 325 shares will receive $325.

When a corporation has been paying ''regular'' quarterly dividends, future distributions usually continue at the same rate. If the company prospers, stockholders can anticipate a dividend increase, and the new ''regular'' quarterly rate will be set somewhat higher.

Note: Common stocks are not required to pay a certain dividend amount, and in fact they are not bound to pay any dividend at all! While preferred stocks (with very few exceptions) have a fixed rate, common stocks entail no such obligation.

Quarterly and Annual Dividend Rates

It is traditional to express a company's common stock dividend as ''so much'' per quarter. To arrive at the company's annual dividend rate, multiply the quarterly rate by 4.

Example: If the current *quarterly* rate is $0.30, then the *annual* rate is $1.20: $0.30 × 4.

This calculation gives the anticipated dividend over the next year. Of course, the dividend could be raised, lowered, or even eliminated during that time. So there is no absolute assurance that the owner of the stock will receive exactly that amount. The annual rate is only an anticipated rate.

Example: Refer to Figure 4-1. The first item listed there is the just-declared "regular" quarterly dividend for Ameriana Bancorp. This dividend of 14 cents ($0.14) will be paid to shareholders of record on September 20. They will receive the dividend on October 4. Since September 20 is a Friday, the ex-dividend will almost certainly be set for Monday, September 16, which is four business days prior to the record date. Interested persons will get additional advance "warning" about this dividend in the Friday, September 13 newspaper, when it will appear in the "Stocks Ex-Dividend September 16" section of the column. This portion of the column is a kind of "last chance to buy the stock if you want the dividend" announcement.

The *annual* dividend rate for Ameriana Bancorp can be determined by multiplying the quarterly rate by four. (Take a few moments to study the footnotes in the figure. Note particularly that "Q" indicates the "quarterly" dividend!)

$$0.14 \times 4 = 0.56 \text{ or } 56 \text{ cents per share}$$

An owner of 100 shares would receive $14 in dividends on October 4—and a total of $56 for the entire year.

SELF-TEST

Use Figure 4-1 to answer the questions in the self-test.

A. What is the *quarterly* dividend rate for PHH Corp?

B. What is the *annual* dividend rate for Standard Products?

C. What amount of dividend would an owner of 300 shares of Yankee Energy Sys receive on September 27th?

ANSWERS TO SELF-TEST

A. $0.30 (30 cents per share)

B. $0.48 (48 cents per share) The quarterly rate is $0.12.

▶ $4 \times .12 = $ ◀ **0.48** or $0.48

C. $120. (300 shares $\times$ $0.40 = $120.)

▶ $300 \times .40 = $ ◀ **120.** or $120

Another source of dividend information is found in a different section of the newspaper. Figure 4-2, from the "New York Stock Exchange Composite Transactions" listing, is one of the most popular sections of the financial press. The "Div" column shows the newspaper's estimate of the stock's *annual* dividend rate.

Figure 4-2
New York Stock Exchange Composite Transactions

52 Weeks Hi	Lo	Stock	Sym	Div	Yld %	PE	Vol 100s	Hi	Lo	Close	Net Chg
18½	10½	BirmghamStl	BIR	.50	3.2	..	235	15⅞	15	15½	...
19¾	8	BlackDeck	BDK	.40	2.1	32	5584	19	18¼	18⅞	– ¾
↓ 38⅛	25½	BlackHills	BKH	1.76	4.6	15	31	38¼	37⅝	38⅛	...
n 10⅜	9⅞	Blackstn1998	BBT	.85	8.4	..	1844	10⅛	10	10⅛	...
n 10⅞	9½	BlackstnAdv	BAT	.98	9.1	..	84	10⅞	10¾	10¾	.
	9⅞	7¾	BlackstnIncTr	BKT	1.00	10.3	..	2103	9⅞	9¾	9¾	...
n 10⅞	9⅞	BlackstnStrat	BGT	.98	9.2	..	1252	10⅝	10½	10⅝	+ ⅛
↑ 10⅝	9⅝	BlackstnTgt	BTT	.95	8.8	..	2696	10¾	10⅝	10¾	+ ⅛
61	36⅞	BlockHR	HRB	1.76	3.0	23	748	59¾	59¼	59⅝	+ ¾
s 15¼	7¾	BlockbstrE	BV			24	6220	11½	11¼	11½	+ ⅛
7¾	5⅛	BluChipValFd	BLU	.73e	9.7	..	201	7½	7¼	7½	+ ⅛
52½	38½	Boeing	BA	1.00	2.0	12	12020	50¼	49¾	50	– ⅛
30¾	19¾	BoiseCasc	BCC	1.52	5.5	..	2104	27⅝	27¼	27¼	+ ⅞
9¾	4	BoltBerNew	BBN	.06	.9	14	270	7	6¾	6⅞	...
7	3	BondInt Gold	BIG			..	30	5½	5½	5½	– ⅛
13¾	7⅞	BordChm un	BCP	1.89e	15.0	..	9	300	12⅝	12½	12⅝	+ ⅛
13¼	7½	BordChm	BCU	1.89e	15.3	..	9	92	12½	12¼	12¾	– ⅛
38¾	27	BordenInc	BN	1.14	3.1	15	1524	36⅜	36	36¼	– ⅛
18⅛	14½	BostCelts	BOS	1.40e	8.1	10	14	17⅜	17¾	17¾	– ¼
↓ 21⅝	16⅝	BostEdsn	BSE	1.58	7.4	13	563	21½	20⅝	21¼	+ ⅜
98¾	87½	BostEdsn pf		8.88	9.0	..	z410	98¾	97¾	...	
16¾	14½	BostEdsn pf		1.46	8.8	..	e		48⅞	48½	– ⅛
...	11¾	CapstdMtg	CMO	2.48	11.7	9	166	21¾	21⅛	21¼	– ¼
19½	10½	CapstdMtg pf		1.60	8.7	.	29	18⅜	18⅛	18⅝	...
2⅜	⁷⁄₃₂	Careercom	CCM			.	164	¾	¹¹⁄₁₆	¹¹⁄₁₆	...
38⅛	26⅝	Carlisle	CSL	1.28	3.9	14	44	32½	32¼	32½	+ ¼
n 11⅛	8½	CarlPlastc	CPA			..	307	8⅞	8¾	8¾	...
10⅞	5⅛	CarolcoPic	CRC			.19	326	6⅛	6¼	6⅜	+ ⅛
↓ 19½	10¼	CarolFrght	CAO	.60	3.0	44	277	20	19¼	19¾	+ ½
49	38	CarolPwr	CPL	3.04	6.4	12	226	47¾	47⅜	47⅜	– ⅜
54⅞	36½	CarpTech	CRS	2.40	4.8	14	67	50¾	50¼	50¼	– ½
5¾	3½	Carriage	CGE	.10	2.3	23	3	4⅜	4¾	4⅜	– ⅛
4½	1	vjCarterHaw	CHH			.33	262	2	2	2	' ...
83⅞	44⅞	CarterWal	CAR	1.00	1.2	24	956	83⅛	81	81⅞	– ⅝
21¾	15¾	CascadeNG	CGC	1.36	6.5	10	58	21	20⅝	20⅞	...
17¾	11½	CashAmInv	PWN	.08	.5	22	348	17¼	16¾	17½	+ ½
n 15	8½	CatellusDev	CDX			.28	1225	10⅝	10⅜	10¾	...
57¾	38⅛	Caterpillar	CAT	1.20	2.5	79	2226	48⅛	47¾	47¾	– ⅜
17½	10½	CedarFair	FUN	1.45	8.8	9	220	16½	16¾	16½	...
36¼	23½	Centel	CNT	.88	3.0	28	912	30	29½	29¾	...
19⅞	15	CentrEngy	CX	1.60	9.3	10	1284	17¼	17	17¼	+ ¼

Dividend rates, unless noted, are annual disbursements based on the last quarterly, semiannual, or annual declaration. Special or extra dividends, special situations or payments not designated as regular are identified by footnotes.

(Courtesy *The Wall Street Journal*, August 30, 1991.)

Examples: Black Hills has an indicated annual dividend of 1.76 ($1.76). An owner of 100 shares of Black Hills would expect to receive a total of $176 in dividends over a year's time.

▶ 100 × 1.76 = ◀ **176.** or $176

Carlisle is listed as paying 1.28 annually ($1.28). A holder of 355 shares of Carlisle would receive $454.40 during the year.

▶ 355 × 1.28 = ◀ **454.4** or $454.40

SELF-TEST

Use Figure 4-2 to answer the self-test.

A. What is the quarterly dividend rate for Caterpillar?

B. What is Black Deck's annual dividend rate?

C. What is the total amount of the dividends a holder of 500 shares of Centel would receive in a year?

ANSWERS TO SELF-TEST

A. $0.30   The question asked for the quarterly rate, so you must divide the annual rate by 4.

▶ 1.20 ÷ 4 = ◀ **0.3** or $0.30

B. $0.40   Shows as ".40" in the Div column.

C. $440.   500 × $0.88 = $440.

▶ 500 × .88 = ◀ **440.** or $440

CHAPTER 5

INTEREST PAYMENTS

While stocks pay dividends, bonds pay interest. A bond is not an equity (ownership) security as are stocks—but rather a *debt* security. A bondholder does not own a "piece" of the business, like a stockholder, but has simply loaned money to the company. The bondholder thus has a creditor-debtor relationship with the corporation. When the bond matures, the bondholder will receive the principal (the "loaned") amount—the face value—and interest payments will cease because the loan will have been repaid.

Semiannual Interest Payments

Until the date on which the bond matures, the company is expected to make regular interest payments on the loan. (There are some exceptions to this, notably with zero-coupon bonds.) While most stocks pay dividends quarterly (four times a year), bonds make interest payments semiannually (twice a year). The months in which payments are made are indicated by the first letters of the months' names, and the months are always six months apart. The day of payment is indicated by a number following the second month's letter.

Examples: A bond's semiannual payments are indicated as "J & J1," which can only refer to January and July because they are exactly six months apart. June and July are only one month apart, and January and June five months apart.

    Interest payments are made on the first of each month: "J1."

"F & A15" indicates interest payments on the 15th of February and August (not February and April because they are only two months apart).

"M & N8" signifies interest payments due on the 8th of May and November. Can you figure out why "M & N" cannot mean March and November?

Most older bonds have interest payment dates of either the first or the fifteenth of the month, but recently issued bonds tend to use a variety of dates.

The Dollar Value of Interest Payment

A bond's interest payment rate is usually shown either as a percent, such as "8.5%," or as "8½s." Both indicate that the bond has an interest rate of 8½% (8.50%) of its par value. A single bond (one bond or 1M) has a par value of $1,000 and, for simplicity's sake, we will do almost all the calculations in the beginning part of this section using one bond as an example. (See Chapter 2, "Pricing Corporate Bonds," for a full explanation of a bond's par value.)

There are several ways to determine the amount of money that will be received, but probably the easiest is to:

- Change the interest rate to its decimal equivalent.
- Move the decimal one place to the right.

(This is the same method we used in Chapter 2 to change a bond's quoted price to its dollar equivalent.)

Example: A bond pays 8½% interest annually. To compute the amount of money that will be received over the year:

- Express the bond's interest rate in decimal format.

$$8½ = 8.5$$

- Move the decimal one place to the right.

$$8.5 \text{ becomes } 85, \text{ or } \$85$$

CALCULATOR GUIDE
Moving the decimal one place to the right is the same as multiplying by 10.

▶ 1 ÷ 2 = ◀ 0.5

then

▶ 8.5 × 10 = ◀ **85.** or $85

Example: A bond with an interest rate of 9¾% pays $97.50 annually. Change 9¾ to 9.75, and then move the decimal one place to the right: $97.50.

CALCULATOR GUIDE

▶ 3 ÷ 4 = ◀ **0.75**

Then

▶ 9.75 × 10 = ◀ **97.5** or $97.50

Since two payments are made annually, each semiannual payment is one-half the annual amount.

Example: If a bond pays $85 in interest annually, one half of this amount is paid every six months. Thus the bondholder receives two payments of $42.50.

CALCULATOR GUIDE

▶ 85 ÷ 2 = ◀ **42.5** or $42.50

Let's figure bond interest on a more realistic number of bonds. Corporate bond "round lots" are ten bonds ($10,000 par or face value). This number of bonds can also be shown as 10M. To arrive at the dollar value of the interest payments on a block of bonds:

- Calculate the single-bond interest payment.
- Multiply the number of bonds by the single-bond interest payment.

Example: A block of 10 bonds (10M or $10,000 par value) with an interest rate of 11⅞% pays total annual interest of $1,187.50

- Calculate the single-bond interest payment. Change 11⅞ to 11.875, and then move the decimal one place to the right. This effectively multiplies the number (11.875) by 10 and gives the annual interest for a single bond, $118.75.
- Multiply the single-bond price ($118.75) by 10 (for 10 bonds) to arrive at $1,187.50. (Or move the decimal one more place to the right.)

CALCULATOR GUIDE

▶ 7 ÷ 8 = ◀ **0.875**

Then

▶ 11.875 × 10 × 10 = ◀ **1187.5** or $1,187.50

Example: $100,000 worth (100M) of 7¼% bonds pays total annual interest of $7,250. Reduce 7¼ to 7.25 and then move the decimal three places to the right. This is equivalent to multiplying by 10 and then by 100!

This "move-the-decimal" method works well for 1, 10, 100, or a million dollars' worth of bonds because you move the decimal 1, 2, 3, or 4 places respectively.

CALCULATOR GUIDE

▶ 1 ÷ 4 = ◀ **0.25**

Then

▶ 7.25 × 10 × 100 = ◀ **7250.** or $7,250

Example: How much interest will be paid by a holding of 25M 12⅛% bonds? First convert the interest rate to a decimal.

12⅛ becomes 12.125

Multiplying by 10 and then by 25 gives interest of $3,031.25

CALCULATOR GUIDE

▶ 1 ÷ 8 = ◀ **0.125**

Then

▶ 12.125 × 10 × 25 = ◀ **3031.25** or $3,031.25

Have you learned to skip that first step yet? It saves a lot of time if you can start with 12.125 rather than having to divide 1 by 8 first.

Example: What annual interest will be paid on a position of 150M 6⅝% bonds?

6⅝ becomes 6.625

Multiplying by 10 and then by 150 gives total annual interest on the position of $9,937.50.

CALCULATOR GUIDE

▶ 5 ÷ 8 = ◀ **0.625**

Then

▶ 6.625 × 10 × 150 = ◀ **9937.5** or $9,937.50

Interest Rates in the Financial News

Figure 5-1 is from the "New York Stock Exchange Bonds" listings section in *The Wall Street Journal*.

- In the listing for the first bond, the "A For P 5s30" bond, the number 5 (just before the letter s) indicates a 5% (5.00) interest rate. The number 30 (just after the letter s) shows that the bond will mature in the year 2030! Traders call these bonds the "fives of 30."

- The third bond listed, AMR 9s16, has an interest rate of 9% (9.00) and will mature in 2016. They are called the "nines of 16."

- The second bond in the right-hand column, CPoM 7¼ 12, has an interest rate of 7¼% (7.25) and will mature in 2012. Note that the letter s is *not* inserted between the interest rate and the maturity date when the interest rate contains a fraction.

Figure 5-1
New York Stock Exchange Bonds

Bonds	Cur Yld	Vol	Close	Net Chg.
CORPORATION BONDS				
Volume, $45,560,000				
AForP 5s30	9.7	10	51½ +	1⅜
AForP 5s30r	9.5	20	52¾ +	1¾
AMR 9s16	9.4	45	95¾ +	⅜
AMR zr06	...	8	40¼ −	¾
AetnLf 8⅛07	8.5	5	95⅜	...
AlaP 9s2000	8.8	5	102	...
AlaP 8¼s03	8.5	22	97⅜ −	1⅛
AlaP 9¾s04	9.3	50	104⅞	...
AlaP 10⅞05	10.5	1	103½ −	1⅛
AlaP 8⅞06	8.9	13	99⅞	...
AlaP 9½08	9.2	25	102⅞ +	⅝
AlskAr 6⅞s14	CV	11	87 −	1¾
AlskAr zr06	...	5	33½	...
AlldC zr98	...	73	54¾ +	⅝
AlldC zr92	...	20	93	...
AlldC zr2000	...	21	45¼	...
AlldC zr03	...	45	33½ +	⅛
AlldC zr09	...	40	19¼ +	⅛
AllgWt 4s98	5.3	11	76	...
AMAX 8½s96	8.5	9	100 +	2
AMAX 9⅜s00	9.3	12	101 +	½
AMAX 8⅝s01	9.0	1	96	...
AMAX 14⅛s94	12.6	10	115 −	½
AMAX 9.23s95	9.3	4	99½	...
ATT 5⅞s95	6.0	29	94⅜ −	1¼
ATT 5⅛s97	6.0	55	91⅜ +	⅝
ATT 4s00	6.0	22	94¼	...

Bonds	Cur Yld	Vol	Close	Net Chg.
Champ 6½s11	cv	3	95½ +	½
CPoM 7¼12	8.7	5	83¾ +	⅛
ChmWst zr10	...	10	31¾	...
C O 4½s92r	4.6	10	98½ +	1/16
Chvrn 8½s95	8.3	10	102 +	½
Chvrn 9⅜s16	9.1	10	103 +	½
Chiquta 11⅞s03	11.3	101	105	...
Chiquta 10½s04	10.7	378	98¼	...
Chiquta 10¼s05	10.5	15	98	...
ChckFul 7s12	cv	114	85 −	¼
ChCft 13s99	12.5	130	103⅝	...
ChryF 9.30s94	10.5	215	88¾ −	¼
ChryF 13¼s99	13.5	135	98 +	⅛
ChryF 12¾s99	13.1	93	97½	...
ChryF 12s92	11.9	2710	031½2 +	15/32
ChryF 7¼s95t	10.2	200	71 −	3
ChryF 8⅜s97	10.9	79	77 +	½
ChryF 8⅛s94	9.3	51	87¾ −	¼
ChryF 7⅝s92	7.7	35	98⅞16 +	1/32
Chrysl 8⅞s95	9.4	45	94¾ +	1
Chrysir 8s98	11.4	14	70½	...
Chrysir 12¾s92	12.7	240	100¼ −	⅜
Chrysir 13s97	15.9	425	82 +	1⅛
Chrysir 12s15	17.5	324	68⅜ +	¼
Chrysir 9.6s94	11.5	810	83½ +	¼
Chrysir 10.95s17	16.7	180	65⅜ +	⅝
Chrysir 10.4s99	15.0	90	69¼ +	¼
ChvrnC 12s94	11.9	100	100⅞	...
v[CircK 7¼s06f	cv	200	8¼	...

(Courtesy of *The Wall Street Journal*, August 30, 1991.)

SELF-TEST

Use Figure 5-1 to answer the questions in the self-test.

A. How much interest would an owner of 50M AetnLf bonds receive in a year?

B. If the 50 bonds referred to in the previous question were sold at the closing price, how much would the seller receive?

C. What is the interest rate, expressed as a decimal, for the Chvrn bonds maturing in 2016?

D. How much interest would a holder of 100M ChckFul bonds receive on each semiannual interest payment date?

E. A client owns a portfolio with the following bond positions:

25M AlaP 9s2000
50M Champ 6½ 11
80M Chiquta 10½ 04

What is the total market value of her bond portfolio?

F. How much interest will be paid annually on the portfolio in question E?

ANSWERS TO SELF-TEST

A. $4,062.50 (8.125 × 10 × 50 = 4062.5 or $4,062.50)

B. $47,687.50 (95.375 × 10 × 50 = 47687.5 or $47,687.50)

C. 9.375% (9⅜ = 9.375)

D. $3,500. The *total annual* interest would be $7,000 (7.0 × 10 × 100 = 7000) but the question asked for the interest to be received on each of the two interest payment dates during the year! The correct answer is half the annual amount, or $3,500!

E. $151,850.

AlaP	25,500	(102 × 10 × 25)
Champ	47,750	(95.5 × 10 × 50)
Chiquta	78,600	(98.25 × 10 × 80)
	$151,850	

F. $13,900.

AlaP	2,250	(9.0 × 10 × 25)
Champ	3,250	(6.5 × 10 × 50)
Chiquta	8,400	(10.5 × 10 × 80)
	$13,900	

CHAPTER 6

ACCRUED INTEREST

When stocks are purchased, they are bought either with the last declared dividend (cum dividend) or without it (ex-dividend). Bonds don't work that way. With very few exceptions (such as zero-coupon bonds, adjustment bonds, and defaulted bonds), bonds trade *with* interest.

Does that mean that, if you sell a bond, you lose the interest earned on it since the last interest payment? No. When you sell a bond, you don't miss out entirely. You, the seller, and the buyer are each entitled to a portion of the next interest payment. You receive from the seller your fair share of the interest payment that will be made on the upcoming payment date, that is, the amount of interest that *accrued* to you while you owned the bond. You are due the interest earned while you owned the bond—and the buyer is entitled to the balance of that interest payment, the part representing the period that the purchaser will have owned the bond.

Settling Bond Trades

When does interest stop accruing to the seller and start accruing to the purchaser? In a transaction involving a corporate or municipal bond, the seller hands over the security sold, and the buyer pays for the security bought, on the settlement date. The seller is entitled to receive interest through the day *before* the trade settles. The buyer, who pays for the bond on settlement date, starts collecting interest on that day. Thus the seller is entitled to receive accrued interest from the time he last received an interest payment through the day before settlement.

Example: On a J & J1 bond, interest payments are made on the first of January and the first of July. (See Chapter 5, "Interest Payments.") If you own this bond and decide to sell it around the end of March, you received the last interest payment on the previous January 1.

But you are entitled to the interest accrued between January 1 through the day before the transaction settles. That accrued interest will be paid to you by the buyer of the bond. The buyer, in turn, will receive the entire July 1 interest payment.

Most trades "settle" on the fifth business day after the trade date. This is true for stocks, corporate bonds, and municipal bonds. (Options and government bonds settle on the next business day after the trade date.)

Example: If you buy a stock on Monday, the trade settles the fifth business day thereafter, which is the following Monday. Tuesday's trades settle the following Tuesday, Wednesday's trades settle the following Wednesday, and so on.

When a legal holiday falls within the settlement period, the settlement day is moved one day forward.

Example: With a legal holiday falling on Friday, a Monday trade settles on Tuesday of the following week.

Figuring Accrued Interest

You can calculate exactly how much accrued interest is due you. The formula for figuring accrued interest on a bond trade is:

$$\text{Accrued Interest} = \text{Annual Interest} \times \frac{\text{Days Since Last Payment Through Day Before Settlement}}{360 \text{ days}}$$

Note: Accrued interest calculations for corporate and municipal bonds use 360-day years and 30-day months.

Example: An 8% corporate bond is purchased, regular way, on January 5. How much accrued interst will be added to the purchase price? The bond pays interest on January 1 and July 1 (J & J1).

A corporate bond trade settles in 5 business days. So this trade will settle on January 12: 5 business days = 1 week.

The seller last received interest on January 1, the previous interest payment day, and is entitled to interest from that day through January 11, the day before settlement. This means the seller should receive 11 days' interest. A full year's interest on an 8% bond would be $80, and the seller "owned" the bond for 11 of the 360 days in the year. He is entitled to that percentage (11/360) of a full year's interest!

$$= \$80 \times \frac{11}{360} = \$2.44$$

See how the formula was derived? This amount, $2.44 of accrued interest, will be paid by the buyer of the bond to the seller of the bond at settlement.

CALCULATOR GUIDE

▶ 8.00 × 10 × 11 ÷ 360 = ◀ **2.4444444**
                                   which we round to $2.44

Note: You can skip the first step—8.00 × 10—if you know that an 8% bond pays total annual interest of $80. The calculation then becomes:

▶ 80 × 11 ÷ 360 = ◀ **2.4444444**

Example: How much accrued interest will be added to a 10M municipal bond trade on November 10th? The bond pays 7% interest and has payment dates of February 1 and August 1.

$$\frac{\text{Accrued}}{\text{Interest}} = \frac{\text{Annual}}{\text{Interest}} \times \frac{\text{Days Since Last Payment Through Day Before Settlement}}{360 \text{ days}}$$

$$= \$70 \times \frac{106}{360} \times 10 = \$206.11$$

The payment date previous to the trade date was August 1. Accrued interest will be calculated from that date through November 16, the day before settlement day. (A November 10 trade settles on November 17.) Accrued interest therefore includes all of August, September, and October—at 30 days each—and 16 days in November, a total of 106 days. We multiplied by 10 because 10 bonds were involved.

CALCULATOR GUIDE

▶ 7.00 × 10 × 106 ÷ 360 × 10 = ◀ 206.11111
                                 which rounds to $206.11

Example: What amount of accrued interest would be added to
a 250M ($250,000) corporate bond trade executed on March
20? The bond has an interest rate of 9½% and interest
payment dates of A & O15.

$$\$95 \times \frac{162}{360} \times 250 = \$10,687.50$$

This is a tricky one. First, did you know that A & O
referred to April and October? We are using the 15th of those
months as payment dates for our example, not the 1st. Since
the trade date, March 20, was after October 15 but before
April 15, we count accrued interest from October 15, the last
payment date. It's easy to miscount the number of days for
which interest is due in October. We "owe" interest from the
15th of October to the end of the month, keeping in mind that
all months are considered to have 30 days. Count the days
off—on your fingers, if necessary. There are 16 days from
the 15th of October to the 30th of October, *inclusive*. Since
the trade date is March 20, the settlement date will be March
27.

Accrued interest is owed for a total of 162 days, as
follows:

Month	Number of Days	Remarks
October	16	October 15 through 30, inclusive
November	30	
December	30	Use only 30-day months for accrued interest figuration on corporate and municipal bonds
January	30	
February	30	
March	26	March 1 through the day before settlement
	162	

CALCULATOR GUIDE

▶ 9.50 × 10 × 162 ÷ 360 × 250 = ◀ **10687.5**
                                  or $10,687.50

Accrued Interest on Government Bonds

Figuring accrued interest on United States government bonds and notes is a bit complicated. Since ''governments,'' as they are called, are traded in much larger blocks than ''munis'' or corporates ($1,000,000 rather than $100,000 or $10,000), the accrued interest calculation must be much more precise. The corporate/municipal rule of 30-day months and 360-day years is not used with governments. *Actual* days are used instead!

In a nonleap year of 365 days, there will be 181 days in the first half of the year and 184 days in the second half of the year. A trade can take place in the first half or the second half of the year, and the number of days in that half-year become the denominator (the number below the line) in the formula. Since we are calculating only a half-year's *time*, we should only use a half-year's *interest*. This difference makes for much more precise, and fairer, accrued interest calculations when dealing with the huge blocks of government bonds that are traded.

Still another difference is that government note and bond trades settle on the *next* business day after the trade date. During nonholiday periods, Monday's trades settle on Tuesday of that same week, Tuesday's trades settle on Wednesday, and so on.

Note: Keep in mind that Friday's trades settle on the following Monday.

The corporate bond accrued interest formula is varied somewhat in that we use one-half a year's interest—and the number of days in the half-year during which the trade took place. Here's the formula:

The main things to remember are:

- Next day settlement rather than fifth business day settlement.

- Actual days in the month and year rather than 30-day months and 360-day years.

- One-half year's interest rather than a full year.

Example: A J & J1 government bond with a 6% interest rate will pay $60 annually in two $30 installments. There are two halves to the bond's ''year''—the period from January 1 through June 30, and the period from July 1 through December 31. Assume a trade date of Wednesday, February 25. The trade settles on Thursday, February 26, and accrued interest is figured through the day before settlement, or February 25. Since the trade took place in the January-July period (not July-January), we use 181 days as the denominator.

$$\frac{\text{Accrued}}{\text{Interest}} = \frac{\text{Semiannual}}{\text{Interest}} \times \frac{\text{Days from Last Payment to Day Before Settlement}}{\text{Days in Trade's Half Year}}$$

$$= \$30 \times \frac{56}{181} = \$9.28 \text{ accrued interest}$$

We owe accrued interest from the last interest payment before the trade, January 1, through the day before settlement. There are 31 days in January, and we accrue interest through the 25 of February. So there are 56 days in the numerator (the number above the line).

CALCULATOR GUIDE

▶ 6.00 × 10 ÷ 2 × 56 ÷ 181 = ◀ **9.2817679** or $9.28

Example: How much accrued interest will be added to a 200M 8% government bond traded on Friday, August 3? The bond's interest-payment dates are M & N1.

The bond was traded in the May-November period (not November-May). So we must count the actual days in that period:

May	31	
June	30	
July	31	
August	31	
September	30	
October	31	
	184	This is the denominator in our formula.

Now we must figure which of the preceding interest days belong to the seller of the bond. The seller is entitled to accrued interest from May 1 (when he last collected interest) to the day before trade settlement. The Friday, August 3, trade settled on the Monday following (the next business day after the trade), August 6. The seller is therefore entitled to 5 days' interest in August—the number of days in the month through the day before settlement. Now we must count up the total number of days we owe the seller:

May	31	
June	30	
July	31	
August	5	
	97	The numerator in our formula.

Now that we have all the pieces, let's put it together. Keep in mind that we are dealing with 200 bonds.

$$\$40 \times \frac{97}{184} \times 200 = \$4,217.39$$

CALCULATOR GUIDE

▶ 8.00 × 10 ÷ 2 × 97 ÷ 184 × 200 = ◀ **4217.3912**
                                    or $4,217.39

SELF-TEST

A. What amount of accrued interest will be added to a trade of 10M corporate 9% bonds sold on March 12? Interest payment dates are J & J1.

B. How much accrued interest will be paid by the buyer of 125M municipal bonds with a 6% interest rate? The trade date is April 10—and interest payment dates are A & O1.

C. What amount of accrued interest is due on a trade of 50M Treasury bonds with a 7% interest rate purchased on Wednesday, June 28. Interest payment dates are M & N1.

ANSWERS TO SELF-TEST

A. $195.

$$\$90 \times \frac{78}{360} \times 10 = \$195.$$

▶ 9.00 × 10 × 78 ÷ 360 × 10 = ◀ **195.** or $195.

Interest accrues from the interest payment date preceding the trade, March 1, through the day before settlement, March 18. Interest is owed the seller for the full months of January and February (at 30 days each) and 18 days in March, a total of 78 days. For corporate bonds and municipal bonds, you must use 30-day months and 360-day years!

B. $333.33

$$\$60 \times \frac{16}{360} \times 125 = \$333.33$$

▶ 6.00 × 10 × 16 ÷ 360 × 125 = ◀ **333.33332** or $333.33

The interest payment dates are April and October 1, and the trade settles on April 17. Only 16 days' interest is due. Again, corporate and municipal bonds use 30-day months and 360-day years.

C. $561.14

$$\$35 \times \frac{59}{184} \times 50 = \$561.14$$

▶ 7.00 × 10 ÷ 2 × 59 ÷ 184 × 50 = ◀ **561.1413**
                                 or $561.14

Interest accrues through the day before settlement. This is a government bond trade so it settles the next business day, the 29th of June. The day before settlement is June 28, so that many days in June are owed, plus the complete month of May. We are using actual days—half a year's interest—and half the total year as the denominator. The May 1-November 1 half-year has 184 days:

May	31
June	30
July	31
August	31
September	30
October	31
	184

Interest is owed from the previous interest payment before the trade, May 1, through the day before settlement, June 28:

May	31
June	28
	59

Note to Series 7 Preparatory Students

Hang in there. This section covers the most difficult math on
the exam. If you got this far and can understand the concept,
you are well on your way to successfully completing the
exam.

The concept of accrued interest and the mathematics it
involves can be formidable. It is important, however, in that
it will be part of your job as a registered representative to be
able to explain the concept to customers. Reps may even be
called upon to prove out the accrued interest figures that
appear on most bond trade confirmations.

The series 7 exam will probably test the subject of accrued
interest, but not exhaustively. You may be asked to figure
actual accrued interest on a small (1M or 10M) corporate or
municipal bond trade, but most probably you will be tested
only on the "actual days" and "next-day settlement" con-
cepts with respect to government bond trades, rather than a
full-blown problem such as that in question C of the self-test.

BORDERS BOOKS & MUSIC #204
2343 E. Lincoln Highway, Langhorne PA
(215) 943-6600

7324   204/0004/04 000510   SALE
ITEM   TX RETAIL DISC SPEC   EXTND
   NYIF VEST POCK GD STOCK BROKER
1 QP 0631568 1 16.95   16.95
                   SUBTOTAL   16.95
    6.000%   TAX1   1.02
1 Item   AMOUNT DUE   17.97
                   CASH   20.00
                   CHANGE DUE   2.03
      01/10/98   01:01 PM
   Thank you for shopping at Borders

CHAPTER 7

CURRENT YIELD

Securities are purchased for investment. Presumably, investing properly will make your money grow—and will help your accumulated capital keep pace with or even outstrip inflation. Many investments are bought without regard for how much money they will bring in, on a regular basis, from dividends or interest. Instead, the investor hopes to have the market value of the investment grow over time so that the securities can be liquidated for a higher price than they were purchased for, that is, for "capital gains." This "buy low-sell high" stategy is sometimes the only one employed, especially by very aggressive traders.

Other investors are concerned with regular income from their investments. Sometimes this is their only concern; sometimes they are striving for a combination of both benefits, capital gains and current income.

In Chapters 7-14, we learn how to measure the continuing income from such investments.

Yield

The concept of "yield" is very important. Investors must be able to determine the amount of yield they receive and compare that yield with the returns (yields) available on alternate investments.

By analogy, farmland is valued in terms of its potential yield. The farmer understandably wants to know how large the harvests will be. The land must be properly prepared and the seed planted. Then a great deal of additional time and effort goes into weeding, watering, and protecting the crops from disease and the ravages of insects. It would be foolish for the farmer to go to all this time, trouble, and expense without a fair degree of assurance that the money to be received from selling the crops will be sufficient to repay him adequately for all the time, trouble, and expense.

An investor should also be able to gauge the expected return from his investment. The "yield" on an investment gives the investor an idea of the *return* to be expected on the investment—what's in it for him. Such returns may be in the form of cash dividends (equity securities—common and preferred stocks) or interest payments (debt securities—bonds). He must then determine whether the expected return is commensurate with the yield that might be earned on alternate investments—and adequate enough to compensate him for the level of risk involved.

Yield is a measure of how much of the money the investor has risked will be returned to him each year in the form of dividends or interest. It shows the percent of the original investment that "returns" to him each year in cash.

Current Yield

One such measurement is known as *current yield,* which is derived by dividing current income by current price. By *current income* we mean the amount of the cash dividend that the stock is expected to pay during the coming year. This calculation shows the percentage "return" for a purchaser of the stock at its current price—the percent of the purchase price that will be returned to the buyer over the coming year. The annual cash dividend is, normally, equal to four times the quarterly rate.

$$\text{Current Yield} = \frac{\text{Annual Dividend}}{\text{Current Price}}$$

Example: XYZ common stock pays a quarterly dividend of $0.30 per share and is selling at 18¼ per share. What is XYZ's current yield?

$$\text{Current Yield} = \frac{\text{Annual Dividend}}{\text{Current Price}}$$

$$= \frac{\$1.20}{\$18.25} = 6.58\%$$

CALCULATOR GUIDE

▶ .30 × 4 ÷ 18.25 × 100 = **6.57534** or 6.58%

Note: We multiply by 100 as the last step to change 0.0657534 in the calculator window (which will show if you press the = button after dividing by 18.25) to 6.57534% (percent). You can eliminate this last step simply by moving the decimal place two spaces to the right, which also converts 0.0657534 to 6.57534% (percent). We'll stick with the "× 100" method for the balance of this text, so that you can read the percentage answer directly from the calculator without moving decimals.

$1.20 is 6.58% of $18.25! It is the investor's return. He will receive in dividends, over the next year, 6.58% of the current price of the stock.

SELF-TEST

Use Figure 7-1 to answer the self-test questions. The *annual* dividend is shown in the "Div" column. Use the "Close" column as the current price. Round your answers to two decimal places.

Figure 7-1
New York Stock Exchange Composite Transactions

52 Weeks Hi	52 Weeks Lo	Stock	Sym	Div	Yld %	PE	Vol 100s	Hi	Lo	Close	Net Chg
125	66⅛	TimeWarner	TWX	1.00	1.2	...	2929	82¼	81⅛	81⅞	+ ⅝
46⅝	29½	TimeWarner pfC		4.38	10.1	...	1787	43⅜	43⅛	43¼	− ¼
49¾	26¾	TimeWarner pfD		5.50	11.4	...	987	48⅝	48¼	48¼	− ⅜
32⅝	21¼	TimesMir	TMC	1.08	3.4	29	1657	31¾	31⅛	31⅜	− ¼
30	20	Timken	TKR	1.00	3.7	52	607	28¾	27⅜	27⅜	−1¼
3⅞	1⅝	Titan	TTN		...	16	76	3⅛	3	3⅛	...
n 6⅝	4	ToddShip	TOD		...	2	127	5¼	5	5	− ⅛
15⅞	**9¾**	**Tokheim**	**TOK**	**.56**	**4.1**	**...**	**281**	**13⅝**	**12⅜**	**13⅝**	**+1⅜**
28½	25¾	ToledoEd pf		2.81	10.3	...	12	27⅜	27⅜	27⅜	...
25¾	22½	ToledoEd pf		2.47e	9.8	...	10	25⅜	25¼	25¼	+ ¼
24⅞	20⅞	ToledoEd pf		2.26e	9.3	...	9	24⅜	24⅜	24⅜	..
26⅞	22⅝	ToledoEd pf		2.36	9.1	...	3	26	26	26	...
25	21	ToledoEd pf		2.21	9.1	...	6	24½	24⅜	24⅜	+ ⅛
8⅝	2¼	Toll Bros	TOL		...	150	451	7¾	7½	7½	...
58½	31	TootsieRoll	TR	.26	.5	23	401	56½	56	56⅛	− ½
58½	38	Torchmark	TMK	1.60	3.1	12	591	51	50⅝	51	+ ¼
20½	11	Toro	TTC	.48	3.1	22	294	16	15⅝	15⅝	− ⅜
25⅞	14½	Tosco	TOS	.60	2.8	4	435	21¾	21⅛	21⅜	− ½
59½	52½	Tosco pf		4.37	7.5	...	4	58	58	58	−1¼
34¾	25¾	TotlSysSvc	TSS	.28e	1.1	31	6	26¾	26⅝	26⅝	− ¼
36	19⅞	ToysRUs	TOY		...	32	5161	34½	33⅝	34½	+ ⅜
4⅜	2	TrammellRE	TCR	.51e	18.5	...	10	2¾	2¾	2¾	− ⅛

(Courtesy of *The Wall Street Journal*, September 5, 1991.)

A. What is the current yield for Torchmark?

B. What is the current yield for Toledo Ed 2.21 preferred?

C. Which has the greatest current yield, Times Mir, Timken, or Tokheim?

ANSWERS TO SELF-TEST

A. 3.14%   ($1.60 ÷ 51 = 3.14%)

▶ 1.60 ÷ 51 × 100 = ◀ **3.13725** or 3.14%

B. 9.07%   ($2.21 ÷ 24.375 = 9.07%)

▶ 2.21 ÷ 24.375 × 100 = ◀ **9.06666** or 9.07%

C. Tokheim

Tokheim: $0.56 ÷ 13.625 = 4.11%

▶ .56 ÷ 13.625 × 100 = ◀ **4.11009** or 4.11%

Timken: $1.00 ÷ 27.375 = 3.65%

▶ 1.00 ÷ 27.375 × 100 = ◀ **3.65296** or 3.65%

Times Mir: $1.08 ÷ 31.375 = 3.44%

▶ 1.08 ÷ 31.375 × 100 = ◀ **3.44223** or 3.44%

Note: You can check your answers, at least to one decimal place, by simply looking at Figure 7-1 under the column headed "Yld %." Try it. Note that the yield (it's the current yield) for:

- Torchmark is 3.1
- Toledo Ed 2.21 pf is 9.1
- Tokheim is 4.1
- Timken is 3.7
- Times Mir is 3.4

All your answers check out! If you round off the answers that we arrived at to just one decimal place, you'll see that they are exactly the same as the yields shown in the newspaper.

Current Yield = Annual Dividend ÷ Market Price

Example: Figure the current yield on a stock that is trading at 78½ and that pays a *quarterly* dividend of $1.35. The annual dividend would, of course, be $5.40 (four times the quarterly rate).

Current Yield = Annual Dividend ÷ Market Price
= $5.40 ÷ 78.5 = 6.88%

▶ 1.35 × 4 ÷ 78.5 × 100 = ◀ **6.87898** or 6.88%

Now refigure the current yield, assuming that the dividend remains the same but the price drops to 67¾ per share.

$5.40 ÷ 67.75 = 7.97%

▶ 1.35 × 4 ÷ 67.75 × 100 = ◀ **7.97047** or 7.97%

The dividend remained the same but the current yield increased. This is logical when you realize that a buyer of the stock at 67¾ *must* be receiving a better return than a buyer at 78½ since they are both receiving the same dividend.

Note: There are inherent weaknesses in the formula used to figure the current yield on common stock. The numerator (the annual dividend) is at best an *estimate* of the total dividends per share that the common stock will pay over the next year. There is nothing certain about the amount of the common stock dividend. It is set by the company's board of directors, and they might very well decide to raise, lower, or even eliminate the expected dividends. If the dividend is changed during the year it will affect the stock's current yield.

Another weakness is that we do not know what the price of the stock will be one year from now! It might go up during that time—or down—and this too will affect the stockholder's return.

We can eliminate one of these weaknesses—the uncertainty of the expected cash flow (dividends or interest) for the coming year—when dealing with *fixed-income* securities such as preferred stocks and bonds. The cash flow on such securities is consistent and is known in advance. There is no "guesswork" as to the amount of annual income that investments in these instruments will generate.

SELF-TEST

A. What is the current yield on a 9% bond trading at 104?

B. What is the current yield on a 6% bond trading at 94½?

ANSWERS TO SELF-TEST

A. 8.65%   ($90 ÷ 1040 = 8.65%)

▶ 9.00 × 10 ÷ 104 × 10 = ◀ **8.653846** or 8.65%

B. 6.35%   ($60 ÷ 945 = 6.35%)

▶ 6.00 × 10 ÷ 94.5 × 10 = ◀ **6.349206** or 6.35%

Note: The 9% bond was selling at a premium. The bond's "nominal" yield is 9.00% (see Chapter 8 for a definition of nominal yield), but its current yield is somewhat less. That bond's current yield *must* be lower than the nominal yield. The only time a bond's nominal yield and its current yield are the same is when the bond is selling for exactly par (100).

Bonds trading at a premium always have a current yield less than their nominal yield, and bonds selling at a discount always have a current yield that is higher than their nominal yield. Note that the 6% bond in question B is trading at a discount, and that its current yield is higher than its nominal yield.

The reason for this is fairly straightforward: A given bond pays a fixed rate of interest—so many dollars each year—whether it is trading in the open market at par, at a premium, or at a discount. The par buyer's nominal and current yield will be the same, but the "lucky" buyer who pays *less* than par will, of course, enjoy a better return. She's getting the same interest payments as the par buyer, but paid less for the bond. By the same token, the buyer who paid more than par for the bond will not fare so well as the others because she "overpaid" for the bond. She receives the same interest as the others but she paid more.

CHAPTER 8

NOMINAL YIELD

Until about 1980, two types of bonds (particularly municipals) were issued—registered and coupon.

- *Registered bonds* have the owner's name, or the name of
an institution holding the bonds for the owner, inscribed
on them. The actual bondholder (the beneficial owner) is
the true owner, whether the bonds are registered directly in
his/her name or in an institution's name (''street name'').
Currently issued bonds come only in the registered form—
or as book-entry, described later.

- *Coupon bonds* (also known as bearer bonds) were not
registered in any name. Like the dollar bills in your wallet,
they were presumed to be the property of the person who
had physical possession of them. The issuing corporation
or municipality had no record of the actual owners—and,
of course, had no way of directly paying the bonds'
semiannual interest directly to these unknown holders.
Interest was collected through the use of ''coupons.''
These coupons—one for each semiannual interest payment over the life of the bond—were attached to the bond
certificate.

Every six months the bondholder (or the institution holding the bonds for the owner) would clip the appropriate
coupon and present it to a bank for cash or deposit. A 30-year
coupon bond had a total of 60 such coupons. The expression
''coupon clipper'' refers to a person whose income is derived
not from strenuous activity, but from the rather pleasant task
of simply cutting coupons from their bearer bonds and pre-
senting them for payment.

Coupon bonds have not been issued for some time, but the many outstanding coupon bonds have not been recalled. Such bonds will trade in the secondary market for another 20 years or so, and there are plenty of them out there! These bonds were so prevalent in the past that the "street" still refers to interest payment dates as "coupon" dates—and to the actual semiannual interest payments as "coupons."

Examples: A bond with an interest rate of 8% is referred to as an "8% coupon" bond. A J & J1 bond is said to have "coupon" dates of January and July 1.

For the balance of this text, we will refer both to a bond's coupon rate and its interest rate interchangeably.

Nominal Yield

A bond's coupon rate (its interest rate) is part of a bond's "name." As such, it is also called the *nominal yield.* The coupon is not influenced by the bond's price or its maturity date; it simply refers to the bond's coupon (interest) rate.

Example: "GM 9s '99" describes a bond with an interest rate of 9% and a maturity date of 1999. The 9% "coupon" rate—expressed to two decimal places as 9.00%—is the bond's nominal yield.

The GM 9s '99 would have a nominal yield of 9.00% whether they were trading at par, at a premium, or at a discount (see Chapter 2). They would have a 9.00% nominal yield whether they had just one year or 20 years to go until maturity.

Knowing a bond's nominal yield enables you to determine the amount of interest paid by the bond. (See Chapter 5 for the formula.)

SELF-TEST

Use Figure 8-1 to answer the self-test questions. Express the nominal yield in "decimal" rather than fractional format.

A. What is the nominal yield for the I Pap 10⅞ 95 bonds?

B. What is the year of maturity for the Intnr bonds with the highest nominal yield?

C. What is the nominal yield for the K mart bonds?

Figure 8-1
New York Exchange Bonds

Bonds	Cur Yld	Vol	Close	Net Chg.
IPap 10⅞95	10.5	1	103½	− ½
Intnr 11s93	11.0	1	100¼	− ¾
Intnr 11½294	11.2	10	103⅛	+ 1
Intnr 11s95	10.6	75	103⅞	+ 2⅛
Jamswy 8s05	cv	100	53	+ 1
vJonsLI 6¾494f	...	1	5¼	− ⅜
vJoneL 9⅞95f	...	5	59½	...
K mart 8⅜17	9.0	44	92⅞	− ⅛
KerrGl 13s96	13.0	5	99¾	+ ¾
KerrMc 7¼12	cv	20	105	− ½
Keycrp 7¾402	8.5	55	90⅞	+ ⅜
KogerP 9¼03f	cv	55	20½	− ½
Kolmrg 8¾409	cv	22	73¼	+ ¼
vLTV 5s88mf	...	35	9½	− ¼
vLTV 13⅞02f	...	10	15	− ½
vLTV 7⅞98f	...	25	7¼	...
vLTV 8¾98f	...	43	7½	...
vLTV Int 5s88f	cv	20	14	− 2
LaQuln 10s02	cv	25	90	...
Leget 6½206	cv	5	103½	− ¾

(Courtesy of *The Wall Street Journal,* September 4, 1991.)

ANSWERS TO SELF-TEST

A. 10.875%   (10⅞, with the fraction expressed as a decimal, equals 10.875)

▶ 7 ÷ 8 = ◀ 0.875

B. 1994   [The 93s and the 95s have a nominal yield of 11.00%—the 94s have a coupon rate of 11.50% (11½).]

C. 8.375%   (8⅜, with the fraction expressed as a decimal, equals 8.375.)

▶ 3 ÷ 8 = ◀ 0.375

Note: Keep in mind that nominal yield is just a fancy way of expressing a bond's stated interest rate, its coupon rate.

CHAPTER 9

YIELD-TO-MATURITY— BASIS PRICING

The most professional measurement of a bond's return is its yield-to-maturity. This is a rather complicated concept involving a bond's *total* return if held to its maturity. It takes into account the purchase price of the bond, its redemption value, the coupon rate, and the length of time remaining to the bond's maturity. Yield-to-maturity utilizes the concept of present value, and assumes that all coupons are reinvested at the yield-to-maturity rate. It is also known as the *internal rate of return*.

Confused? In plainer English, yield-to-maturity is the truest measure of the return that a bond investor would receive by holding the bond to its maturity. Under these conditions, all cash inflows (the interest payments during the life of the bond and the principal payment at maturity) and expenses (the cost of the bond) can be precisely calculated in advance. Since we are dealing with a fixed-income security, there is no uncertainty about the amount of income to be received (as there would be with a common stock). And the ultimate "sale" price for the security (the return of principal) is also known; if the bond is held until maturity, the issuing corporation will redeem it at par, $1,000. Isn't this the same, in financial terms, as simply "selling" the bond at par?

This yield calculation even factors in the difference between the par value of the bond and its purchase price. For example, if you pay less than par for a bond and hold it to maturity, you will then receive a full $1,000; the yield-to-maturity figures in these additional funds. If you pay a premium price for a bond—more than the par value you will receive at maturity—this "loss" is also taken into account.

When figuring nominal yield, we ignore the bond's price and its maturity date. When figuring current yield, we factor in the bond's purchase price (current price) and again disregard the length of time to maturity. When dealing with yield-to-maturity, we factor in all these elements.

We know:

- The price of the bond—its current price.
- When and in what amounts interest will be received—the semiannual interest payments.
- The "sale" price—$1,000 at maturity.

Factoring in all these elements, using present values, and even accounting for the reinvestment of interest payments as they are received gives us yield-to-maturity, the most professional way of figuring yield on long-term debt instruments.

Example: While bonds are sometimes quoted as a percent of par, such as 98½ or 102¾, most professionals quote bonds, especially municipals, on a "yield" basis—at the bond's yield-to-maturity. As we shall soon explain, a 10-year 9% bond trading at 96 can also be quoted on a 9.63 "basis." This means that a bond with a 9% coupon, trading at a current price of 96 ($960) and maturing in 10 years, has a yield-to-maturity of 9.63%.

How, then, is yield-to-maturity computed? There are several ways to determine a bond's true yield-to-maturity. This chapter demonstrates the use of the yield basis book. Chapter 10 shows the "rule-of-thumb" method.

The Yield Basis Book

The most commonly employed methods include using either a "yield basis" book or a programmable calculator. A simplified page from a "basis" book is reproduced in Figure 9-1. Most basis books are a lot more detailed than this sample page. They would be in increments of single or half-years rather than five years, and the price column might be in half-point increments rather than the two-point increments illustrated. But the page as shown is more than adequate for our purposes.

Figure 9-1
Sample Page from a Bond Yield "Basis" Book

| | | 9% COUPON | | |
Price	5 Years	10 Years	15 Years	20 Years
92.00	11.13	10.30	10.04	9.93
94.00	10.58	9.96	9.77	9.68
96.00	10.04	9.63	9.51	9.45
98.00	9.51	9.31	9.25	9.22
100.00	9.00	9.00	9.00	9.00
102.00	8.50	8.70	8.76	8.79
104.00	8.01	8.40	8.52	8.58
106.00	7.54	8.11	8.29	8.38
108.00	7.07	7.83	8.07	8.18

The quotations in Figure 9-1 would be used for bonds with a 9.00% nominal yield (a 9% coupon), and for bond prices in the 92 to 108 range with maturities from 5 to 20 years. A "real" yield book would have different pages for other coupon rates such as 8⅞% and 9⅛%, and each page would include many more figures than our sample.

A basis book may be used to convert a bond's price to its yield-to-maturity—or its yield-to-maturity to a price. A bond's price is a dollar amount, expressed as a percent of the bond's par value. A bond priced at 98¼ would sell for $982.50; a bond quoted at a price of 103⅜ would be worth $1033.75. A bond's yield-to-maturity is a percent. (See Chapter 2 for bond pricing.) A bond with a 7.58 "basis" has a yield-to-maturity of 7.58%.

Converting Price to Yield-to-Maturity

Example: What is the yield-to-maturity for a 10-year bond with a 9% coupon offered at 94? In Figure 9-1, locate the bond's price in the first column, and then read along that line two places to the right. Now you are looking at the intersection of the 94.00 PRICE line and the 10 YEARS time to maturity line. That intersection reads "9.96," which is the bond's yield-to-maturity, 9.96%.

An investor paying 94 ($940) for the bond and holding it until it matures would have a yield-to-maturity on her investment of 9.96%. Note that the bond is trading at a discount, and, as with current yield, the yield-to-maturity on discount bonds will always be higher than the bond's nominal yield.

- This bond's nominal yield (its coupon rate) is 9.00%.
- This bond's current yield is 9.57% ($90 ÷ 940 = 9.57%).

CALCULATOR GUIDE

▶ 9.00 × 10 ÷ 94 × 10 = ◀ **9.574468** or 9.57%

- This bond's yield-to-maturity is 9.96% (from the yield table). The current yield is higher than the nominal yield because you are factoring in the relatively low price (a discount) you paid for the bond in return for the interest payments. The yield-to-maturity is higher yet because you are also taking into account the fact that more money will be repaid to the buyer at maturity ($1,000) than was paid for the bond ($940).

Example: What is the yield-to-maturity for a 20-year 9% bond priced at 106? In Figure 9-1, read down the PRICE column until you hit 106.00. Then scan over four columns to the right (the 20 YEARS column) to a yield-to-maturity of 8.38% An investor paying 106 ($1,060) for the bond and holding it until it matures would have a yield-to-maturity on his investment of 8.38%.

Since the bond is trading at a premium, both its current yield and its yield-to-maturity will be below its nominal yield.

- This bond's nominal yield is 9.00% (its coupon rate).
- This bond's current yield is 8.49% ($90 ÷ 1060 = 8.49%).

CALCULATOR GUIDE

▶ 9.00 × 10 ÷ 106 × 10 = ◀ **8.490566** or 8.49%

- This bond's yield-to-maturity is 8.38% (from the yield table).

Since we are dealing with a bond selling at a premium, we know that both its current yield and its yield-to-maturity will be smaller than its nominal yield. The current yield is lower than the coupon rate (nominal yield) because the bond was bought for greater than its par value. The yield-to-maturity is still lower reflecting the fact that the investor will buy for $1,060 but will only get back $1,000 when the bond matures.

Converting Yield-to-Maturity to Price

Example: What is the price of a 9% 15-year bond selling at a
9.51 basis? In Figure 9-1, run down the 15 YEARS column
until you hit the 9.51 figure. Then scan to the left, all the way
to the PRICE column, and find the price of 96.00. The price
for a 9.51 basis bond is 96.00, which, expressed in dollars,
comes to $960 per bond.

Note that the basis, 9.51, is higher than the coupon rate. This
indicates that the bond must be selling at a discount. If a
buyer earns more than the coupon rate, he is buying the bond
for less than its par value.

Example: What is the price for a 9% 5-year bond selling at a
7.07 basis? In Figure 9-1, go down the 5 YEARS column
until you hit the 7.07 figure. Then scan all the way to the left
to find the price of 108. That price equals $1,080 per bond, a
premium price. Since a buyer would have to pay more than
par to buy this bond, he would receive a yield of less than the
coupon rate.

Note: The yield shown for Treasury bonds and notes in the
newspaper listings (in the "Ask Yld." column) is yield-to-
maturity (see Figure 3-2, page 17). The yield shown in the
newspaper listings for corporate bonds is current yield (see
the "Cur Yld" column in Figure 2-1, page 10). Many
municipal bonds, especially serial bonds, are quoted on a
yield basis rather than at specific dollar prices. That yield
basis is yield-to-maturity. More on this later in Chapter 11.

Interpolating the Yield Basis Book

The basis book works fine when you are converting a price to
a yield, and the exact bond price is listed in the table. But
what do you do when the price isn't listed? That's when you
must interpolate. *Interpolation* is the method of estimating an
unknown number that is between two known numbers.

Figure 9-2 is a small portion of Figure 9-1. Let's use a
little piece of the table we have been practicing on. We can
see immediately that a 9% 5-year bond priced at 94.00 has a
yield-to-maturity of 10.58%, and that a 9% bond priced at
96.00 has a yield-to-maturity of 10.04%

But what about a bond priced at 95.00? The 95 price is
exactly half-way (50% of the way) between the prices of 94

Figure 9-2

	9% Coupon	
Price	5 Years	
94.00	10.58	
96.00	10.04	

and 96. So we assume that the yield-to-maturity for a bond at that price will be half-way (50% of the way) between the 9.96 and 9.63 basis prices. There is a difference of 0.54 between 10.58 and 10.04 (10.58 − 10.04 = 0.54). 50% of that difference is 0.27 (0.5 × 0.54).

Note that as the prices go up, the yields go down. Therefore we have to lower the 10.58 basis price by 0.27, reducing it to 10.31 (10.58 − 0.27 = 10.31). That gives us the yield-to-maturity for a bond priced at 95, a 10.31% basis.

To solve more difficult examples, it is necessary to establish a proportion. A *proportion* is an equality between ratios. These are fairly simple to do.

Example: In the previous example, we would say that "1 is to 2 as x is to 0.54." The x is what we are looking for, the amount we have to subtract from the 10.58 yield for a bond trading at 94 to arrive at the yield for a bond trading at 95.

Let's identify all the figures used in the computation.

- 1 is the difference between the 94 and 95 bond prices.
- 2 is the difference between the 94 and 96 prices.
- The unknown quantity (x) is the difference between the 10.58 yield and the figure we are seeking.
- 0.54 is the entire difference between 10.58 and 10.04.

To solve the problem, we multiply the "outside" numbers (1 × 0.54), and then divide by the known "inside" number (2).

$$(1 \times 0.54) \div 2 = 0.27$$

CALCULATOR GUIDE

▶ 1 × 0.54 ÷ 2 = **0.27** ◀

We then subtract the figure derived, 0.27, from 10.58 to arrive at our answer of 10.31. That's the yield-to-maturity for a bond priced at 95.00

SELF-TEST

Use Figure 9-1 to answer the following questions.

A. What is the yield-to-maturity for a 15-year 9% bond trading at 98?

B. What is the yield-to-maturity for a 10-year 9% bond trading at par?

C. What is the yield-to-maturity for a 5-year 9% bond trading at 103?

D. What is the yield-to-maturity for a 20-year 9% bond trading at 104½?

ANSWERS TO SELF-TEST

A. 9.25%
Go down the 15 YEARS column and across the 98.00 line and read the answer where the lines intersect: 9.25.

B. 9.00%
We really don't need the chart to solve this one as bonds trading at par (100) have a current yield and a yield-to-maturity that are exactly equal to their nominal yield. But check it out on the chart anyway. Go down the 10 YEARS column until it intersects with the 100.00 line. There's the answer: 9.00%.

C. 8.26%
The precise answer is 8.255%, which can be rounded off to 8.26%. The answer can be "eyeballed" if you realize that the yield you are looking for is half-way between the 102 and 104 prices, and therefore the answer is to be found half-way between their respective yields. The half-way point between 8.50 and 8.01 is 8.255 (8.50 + 8.01 ÷ 2 = 8.255).

Let's also solve this one the "proper" way by setting up a proportion. (That's what you have to do when dealing with more complex problems anyway.) The proportion sets up this way:

1 is to 2 as x is to 0.49

- 1 is the difference between the 102 price and the price we are looking for, 103.

- 2 is the difference between the two *prices* on either side of the price we are seeking, 102 and 104.

- x is the figure we must subtract from the 8.50 yield to reduce it to the yield for a 103 price.
- 0.49 is the difference between 8.50 and 8.01, the *yields* on either side of the yield we are looking for.

To solve, we multiply the two outside numbers and divide by the known inside number. The outside numbers in the proportion are 1 and 0.49. The known inside number is 2; so we multiply 1 and 0.49 and then divide by 2.

$$1 \times 0.49 \div 2 = 0.245$$

That's the amount we must subtract from the 8.50 yield to arrive at the yield for a bond priced at 103.

$$8.50 - 0.245 = 8.255$$

D. 8.53%
Here's the proportion:

$$0.50 \text{ is to } 2 \text{ as } x \text{ is to } 0.20$$

Multiplying the outside numbers and then dividing by the known inside number gives 0.05 (0.50 × 0.20 ÷ 2 = 0.05). We then subtract that number from 8.58: 8.58 − 0.05 = 8.53.

If you did not follow the explanation, here's where all the numbers came from:

- The prices bracketing the price we are seeking are 104 and 106. The difference between these two numbers is 2.
- The difference between the first number, 104, and the price we are looking for, 104.50, is 0.50.
- The difference between the yields for 104 and 106 is 0.20: 8.58 − 8.38.

CHAPTER 10

THE RULE-OF-THUMB YIELD-TO-MATURITY

The yields in the previous chapter's Figure 9-1 are the same as the yields that would be obtained through the use of a calculator programmed for the figuration of such yields. But what if you are trying to figure a yield-to-maturity and you haven't a basis book or a properly programmed calculator at hand? You can arrive at an approximation of a bond's yield-to-maturity through the rule-of-thumb method. This may be sufficient for your purposes, but keep in mind that the yield obtained is at best an approximation. It is not the exact yield-to-maturity, but merely "in the ballpark." One should use either a bond calculator or the basis book if available; the rule-of-thumb method should only be used when you are "out in the field" and haven't the proper tools available!

The formula for the rule of thumb yield-to-maturity is a variation of the current yield formula.

$$R \text{ of } T \text{ YTM} = \frac{\text{Annual Interest} \begin{array}{c} + \dfrac{\text{Discount}}{\text{Years to Maturity}} \\ \text{or} \\ - \dfrac{\text{Premium}}{\text{Years to Maturity}} \end{array}}{(\text{Current Price} + \$1{,}000) / 2}$$

Notice that the numerator takes into account that the bond might be purchased at either a discount or a premium. Since all bonds are redeemed at par when they mature, the calculation takes into account:

- Either the "extra" money that will eventually be earned by the bondholder if he buys the bond at a discount.

- Or the money that will be lost when a bond is bought at a premium.

This profit or loss is "spread" over the years to maturity as an addition to, or a subtraction from, the interest payments. This makes sense.

- An investor buying a bond at a discount (below 100) has two sources of income: the semiannual interest payments and the additional income that she will eventually receive (the difference between her purchase price of less than $1,000 per bond and the $1,000 the issuer will pay her when the bond matures).

- The investor buying a bond at a premium (above 100) will eventually suffer a loss when the bond matures. Having paid more than par for the bond, she will only receive $1,000 from the issuer at maturity. That's why we subtract the premium from the interest payments; it reflects that loss.

Therefore, in the numerator (the numbers above the fraction line):

- The discount earned, annualized, is *added* to the annual interest.

- Any premium, annualized, is *subtracted* from the annual interest.

Note: Annualized means spread out over the years to maturity. We annualize by dividing the premium or discount by the number of years to maturity. That's why in the formula the discount or premium is divided by the number of years to maturity.

The denominator, taken from the current yield formula, is changed in that we use the *average* of the current price and the bond's value at maturity (always $1,000). That's why the sum of the bond price and its par value is divided by 2.

Example: What is the rule-of-thumb yield-to-maturity for a 7% 10-year bond trading at 94?

$$\text{R of T YTM} = \frac{\text{Annual Interest} + \dfrac{\text{Discount}}{\text{Years to Maturity}}}{(\text{Current Price} + \$1{,}000) / 2}$$

$$= \frac{\$70 + \dfrac{\$60}{10}}{(\$940 + \$1{,}000)/2} = \frac{\$70 + \$6}{\$1{,}940/2} = \frac{\$76}{\$970} = 7.84\%$$

CALCULATOR GUIDE

▶ 100 + 94 ÷ 200 M+ 100 − 94 ÷ 10 + 7 ÷ Mrc
                               = ◀ **7.8350515** or 7.84%

Note: "M+" indicates the memory plus button on the calculator. "Mrc" indicates the memory recall button. This calculator guide was developed by the author (with the able and necessary assistance of Doug Carroll) as a one-step method that enables the student to calculate the yield without having to write down any of the intermediate numbers.

With this method it is also unnecessary to change a bond's quoted price or coupon rate into their dollar equivalents. You simply:

- Add 100 and the bond's quoted price (expressing any fraction in decimal form).
- Divide by 200.
- Enter into memory.

The bond's quoted price is subtracted from 100 and then divided by 10 plus the bond's coupon rate. As with the bond's price, any fraction in the coupon rate should be expressed as a decimal.

CALCULATOR GUIDE—ALTERNATE METHOD
If you are comfortable with the conversion of a bond's price and coupon rate into dollars, use this calculator guide.

▶ 940 + 1000 ÷ 2 M+ 60 ÷ 10 + 70 ÷ Mrc × 100
                               = ◀ **7.83505** or 7.84%

- 940 is the bond's quoted price, expressed in dollars.
- 60 is the dollar difference between the cost of the bond and its redemption value (1,000 − 940).
- 70 is the annual interest rate, in dollars.

The previous example used a bond selling at a disount. The amount of the annualized discount was added to the interest income. The next example uses a premium bond, and we will have to subtract the annualized premium from the interest income.

Example: What is the rule-of-thumb yield-to-maturity for a 9½% 12-year bond selling at 106?

$$\text{R of T YTM} = \frac{\text{Annual Interest} - \dfrac{\text{Premium}}{\text{Years to Maturity}}}{(\text{Current Price} + \$1{,}000) \,/\, 2}$$

$$= \frac{\$95 - \dfrac{\$60}{\$12}}{(\$1{,}060 + \$1{,}000)/2} = \frac{\$95 - \$5}{\$2{,}060/2} = \frac{\$90}{\$1{,}030} = 8.74\%$$

CALCULATOR GUIDE

▶ 100 + 106 ÷ 200 M+ 100 − 106 ÷ 12 + 9.50 ÷ Mrc
                              = ◀ **8.737864** or 8.74%

CALCULATOR GUIDE—ALTERNATE METHOD
This alternate method is for calculators without a reverse-sign [+/−] key.

▶ 1060 + 1000 ÷ 2 M+ 60 ÷ 12 = (5)
ON/C 95 − 5 ÷ Mrc × 100 = ◀ **8.73786** or 8.74%

After dividing by 12 and pressing the equals (=) button, the calculator window shows 5. You must remember this number—we show it as (5)—and subtract it from the bond's coupon rate (95 − 5) after you clear the calculator's last entry by pressing "ON/C." This extra step is necessary when working with a premium-priced bond and you are using a calculator without a reverse-sign (+/−) key.

If your calculator does have such a key, use the following method.

CALCULATOR GUIDE—ALTERNATE METHOD
This alternate method is for calculators without a reverse-sign [+/−] key.

▶ 1060 + 1000 ÷ 2 M+ 60 ÷ 12 = +/− + 95 ÷ Mrc ×
100   = ◀ **8.73786** or 8.74%

SELF-TEST

A. What is the rule-of-thumb yield-to-maturity for a 20-year bond with a 12% coupon trading at 94?

B. What is the rule-of-thumb yield-to-maturity for a bond with a 7% coupon rate, 10 years to maturity, and a price of 107¼?

ANSWERS TO SELF-TEST

A. 12.68%
A 12% bond pays annual interest of $120. The price of 94 ($940) represents a $60 discount, which, annualized

over 20 years, adds $3 to the numerator. A 12% bond trading at a discount must have a current yield and a yield-to-maturity greater than its coupon rate.

$$= \frac{\$120 + \dfrac{\$60}{\$20}}{(\$940 + \$1,000)/2} = \frac{\$120 + \$3}{\$1,940/2} = \frac{\$123}{\$970} = 12.68\%$$

▶ 100 + 94 ÷ 200 M+ 100 − 94 ÷ 20 + 12 ÷ Mrc
= ◀ **12.680412** or 12.68%

- 94 is the bond's price.
- 20 represents the years to maturity.
- 12 is the coupon rate.

Alternate Method

▶ 940 + 1000 ÷ 2 M+ 60 ÷ 20 + 120 ÷ Mrc × 100
= ◀ **12.68041** or 12.68%

B. 6.06%

$$= \frac{\$70 - \dfrac{\$72.50}{\$10}}{(\$1,072.50 + \$1,000)/2} = \frac{\$70 - \$7.25}{\$2,072.50/2}$$

$$= \frac{\$62.75}{\$1,036.25} = 6.606\%$$

A 7% bond pays $70 in annual interest. The price of 107¼ ($1,072.50) represents a $72.50 premium, which, annualized over 10 years, subtracts $7.25 from the numerator. Since the bond is trading at a premium, it is to be expected that the yield-to-maturity will be below the bond's coupon rate.

▶ 100 + 107.25 ÷ 200 M+ 100 − 107.25 ÷ 10 + 7 ÷ Mrc
= ◀ **6.0554885** or 6.06%

This method is for calculators equipped with a reverse-sign (+/−) key.

▶ 1072.50 + 1000 ÷ 2 M+ 72.50 ÷ 10 = +/− + 70 ÷
Mrc × 100 = ◀ **6.05548** or 6.06%

Let's review the CALCULATOR GUIDE instructions:

	Cost			Cost	Years to
▶ 100 +	Price	÷ 200 M+	100 −	Price	÷ Maturity +
Coupon	÷ Mrc = ◀				

With this method you do not have to convert numbers other than to express any fractions in the bond's price or coupon rate as a decimal.

- A cost price of 87 is entered exactly that way: 89½ is entered as 89.5; 103⅜ is entered as 103.375, and so on.

- Similarly, the coupon is plugged in directly: A coupon rate of 9% is entered as 9, a rate of 7½ as 7.5, 11⅞ as 11.875, and so on.

Note that the answer reads directly as a percent: 6.85 = 6.85%, 9.19 = 9.19%, etc. If you can work directly from the rule-of-thumb formula, fine. If not, we suggest you follow the Calculator Guide method previously described. It works!

CHAPTER 11

PRICING MUNICIPAL BONDS

Municipal bonds are priced in two ways:

1. As a percent of their par value.
2. On a yield-to-maturity basis.

Munis (formerly called "tax-exempts") are usually issued either as term bonds or serial bonds. *Term bonds* are priced according to the first method (as a percent of par). *Serial bonds* are quoted on a yield-to-maturity basis.

Percent of Par Pricing

A quick review of Chapter 2 might be in order here, since the method for pricing term municipal bonds is exactly the same as that used for pricing corporate bonds. Term bonds priced in this fashion are sometimes called "dollar bonds." Prices are expressed in points and eighths such as 98¼, 97⅞, 102, 103½, etc. As with corporate bonds, we can use either of two methods to convert these "quotes" into dollars and cents.

Method 1: First convert any fractional part of the bond's quote into decimal format.

Example: 102½ becomes 102.5, 97⅜ becomes 97.375, etc.

Then multiply by ten.

Example: 102.5 × 10 = $1,025 and 97.375 × 10 = $973.75

Method 2: First convert any fractional part of the bond's quote into decimal format.

Example: 102½ becomes 102.5, 97⅜ becomes 97.375, etc.

Then move the decimal point one place to the right: 102.5 becomes 1025. or $1,025; 97.375 becomes 973.75 or $973.75.

Either method gives the dollar value of a single bond (1M) at the quoted price. For larger blocks of bonds, multiply the single bond dollar value by the number of bonds involved.

The quotes should be thought of as having "percent of par value" written after them!

Example: A bond quoted at 98¾ means that it is trading at 98¾% of its par value. A bond quoted at 104⅝ is trading at 104⅝% of its par value.

Learn to think of a term bond's price in terms of its par value. Bonds are traded at par (100), at a discount (less than 100), or at a premium (more than 100).

- Sometimes bonds are trading at a quoted price of exactly 100. We call this price "par."
- A bond selling at any price below 100 is selling for less than its face value of $1,000 per bond. These are discount prices.
- Bonds selling at prices above 100 are trading for more than their face value—more than $1,000 per bond. These are premium prices.

Example: The dollar value of 10 bonds (10 M) trading at 102½ is $10,250.

102.5 × 10 = $1,025.   (the dollar value of *one* bond at 102½)

Note: You can also move the decimal in 102.5 one place to the right:

1,025 × 10 = $10,250.   (the dollar value of *10* bonds at 102½)

CALCULATOR GUIDE

▶ $102.5 \times 10 \times 10 =$ ◀ **10250.** or $10,250.

Example: What is the dollar value of 150 bonds (150 M) trading at 97⅜? The answer is $146,062.50

$$97.375 \times 10 = \$973.75$$

(Or just move the decimal in 97.375 one place to the right.) Then multiply by the number of bonds (150), for a total of $146,062.50.

$$973.75 \times 150 = \$146,062.50$$

CALCULATOR GUIDE

▶ $97.375 \times 10 \times 150 =$ ◀ **146062.5** or $146,062.50

Yield-to-Maturity Pricing

While "term" municipal bonds are usually quoted like corporate bonds (as a percent of par), municipal serial bonds are most often quoted at basis prices, which express their yield to maturity rather than their actual price in dollars. Whereas a term bond quote might read "98⅛" or "105¾," serial bond quotes might be "6.05" or "7.13."

Example: A quoted offering price of 6.05 means that a (serial) bond bought at that price will have a yield to maturity of 6.05%. The 7.13 bond is being offered to yield (yield to maturity) 7.13%.

Most institutional buyers are not particularly concerned with the specific price they pay for a bond. They feel it is unimportant whether they pay premium or discount prices. What is important to them is the yield they will receive from the investment—what's in it for them! This is best expressed in the bond's yield to maturity, which takes into account the bond's interest payments, length to maturity, and any discount or premium. (Review Chapter 10 for more details on this subject.)

Basis prices are figured using either the yield basis tables or a calculator equipped to figure yields to maturity. The "tombstones" on new issues of serial bonds usually show each bond's "price" as a yield. Traders deal in such bonds on a yield basis.

Example: A quote might say "7.21 bid—offered at 7.19." The bid looks higher than the asked (7.21 vs. 7.19), but it actually represents a lower price. The quote is for a bond having a 7.00% nominal yield (a 7% coupon). Assume the bond will mature in, say, 10 years and the actual dollar value for a 7.21 bid is $985 (a price of 98½). That's the amount the bidder is willing to pay—$985 a bond—which gives him a yield to maturity of 7.21% at that price. The seller is asking for more dollars (isn't that what sellers do?) and wants 98⅝ ($986.25) per bond. If the buyer meets that higher price, he will be getting a yield to maturity of only 7.19%.

This is logical since the higher the price paid for the bond, the lower the yield to maturity will be. The bond has a fixed interest rate—all buyers receive the same interest—so that the lower the price paid for the bond, the higher the return!

Example: The following quote appears both as a percent of par and as a yield to maturity:

Bid	Asked	
98½	98⅝	(percent of par pricing)
7.21	7.19	(yield-to-maturity pricing)

Since both sides of the quote are yields to maturity of more than 7.00%, obviously the bond is being quoted at discount prices.

- Discount prices always give current yields and yields to maturity that are higher than the bond's nominal yield. The higher price gives the lower yield to maturity.

- Premium prices always give current yields and yields to maturity that are lower than the bond's coupon rate.

Example: The same bond (10 years to maturity—7% coupon), quoted at premium prices, might look like this:

Bid	Asked	
104¼	104½	(percent of par pricing)
6.41	6.38	(yield-to-maturity pricing)

SELF-TEST

A. What is the dollar cost for a block of $25,000 par value term municipal bonds trading at 94⅛?

Use the following information to answer questions B and C.

A municipal serial bond with a 6% coupon is quoted "6.01—5.99."

B. Does the bid represent a premium or discount price?

C. Does the offer represent a premium or discount price?

D. What is the value, in dollars and cents, for a block of 100 (100M) municipal term bonds trading at 101⅝?

ANSWERS TO SELF-TEST

A. $23,531.25   (94.125 × 10 × 25 = $23,531.25)

▶ 94.125 × 10 × 25 = ◀ **23531.25** or $23,531.25

B. A discount price
Since the bid yield of 6.01% is higher than the coupon rate of 6.00%, the bond is being bid for at a price of less than par. The "less than par price" gives a higher than coupon rate yield.

C. A premium price
The offering yield of 5.99 indicates a dollar price of more than par. Premium prices always translate into yields of less than the coupon rate.

D. $101,625.   (101.625 × 10 × 100 = $101,625.)

▶ 101.625 × 10 × 100 = ◀ **101625.** or $101,625.

CHAPTER 12

COMPARING TAX-FREE AND TAXABLE YIELDS

Equivalent Taxable Yield

The interest payments on corporate and Treasury bonds are taxable by the federal government, but the interest on most municipal bonds is exempt from federal taxation. This poses a question for the investor trying to compare the yields on taxable and tax-exempt securities: How can the yield on a tax-free municipal bond be compared with the yield on a taxable investment?

The answer is that investors must compare the dollars they get to keep after taking taxes into consideration. While the dollars of interest earned on a corporate or government bond may be greater than the interest received on a municipal bond, it is necessary to compute how these dollars of interest would compare *after* accounting for the tax payments due on the corporate/government investments. The total interest payments may be greater on the taxable bonds, but the investor must pay federal tax on these amounts, while the municipal bond investor gets to keep the full interest.

The formula used to convert the yield on a tax-exempt municipal issue to the comparable after-tax yield on a taxable issue provides investors with what is known as the *equivalent tax yield*. This calculation permits investors to compare yields on a ''fair'' basis, taking federal taxes into account. After all, investors should be interested in the dollars of interest they get to *keep*.

$$\text{Equivalent Taxable Yield} = \frac{\text{Tax-Exempt Yield}}{1. - \text{Tax Bracket Percent}}$$

Example: For an investor in the 28% tax bracket, a tax-exempt yield of 6.25% is equivalent to a taxable yield of 8.68%

$$\text{Equivalent Taxable Yield} = \frac{\text{Tax-Exempt Yield}}{1. - \text{Tax Bracket Percent}}$$

$$= \frac{6.25}{1. - 0.28} = \frac{6.25}{0.72} = 8.68\%$$

Note: In the denominator (the bottom number), you must express the investor's tax bracket in decimal form. Thus a 28% tax bracket is entered as 0.28, a 33% tax bracket is written as 0.33, etc.

The calculation shows that the investor would receive the same amount of after-tax dollars from a tax-free municipal bond with a yield of 6.25% as he would from a taxable bond with a yield of 8.68%.

CALCULATOR GUIDE

▶ 1 − 0.28 M+ 6.25 ÷ Mrc = ◀ **8.6805555** or 8.68%

This formula may be used by an investor who is being offered a municipal bond with a yield-to-maturity of 6.25%. If he is thinking of switching some of his taxable bond holdings into munis, he must appreciate that he will be losing ground, interest-wise, if he sells any of his corporate bonds that yield 8.68% or more. If that investor owns 8.68% corporates, he will earn the same number of dollars after taxes with a muni bond yielding 6.25%, and more after taxes with a muni bond yielding more than 6.25%

Finding the Equivalent Tax-Exempt Yield

The formula can be worked "backwards." That is, given an investment with a taxable yield, what tax-exempt yield will result in the same number of dollars "in the pocket"? In this case, we start with a corporate or government bond yield and ask, "What yield-to-maturity do we have to earn on a tax-exempt to earn the same after-tax interest?" After all, quality considerations aside, the investor is primarily interested in earning as much after-tax income as possible.

$$\begin{array}{c}\text{Tax-Exempt}\\\text{Yield}\end{array} = \begin{array}{c}\text{Taxable}\\\text{Yield}\end{array} \times (1. - \text{Tax Bracket Percent})$$

Example: For an investor in the 33% tax bracket, a taxable yield of 9.84% is equivalent to a tax-exempt yield of 6.59%.

$$\begin{array}{c}\text{Tax-Exempt}\\\text{Yield}\end{array} = \begin{array}{c}\text{Taxable}\\\text{Yield}\end{array} \times (1. - \text{Tax Bracket Percent})$$
$$= 9.84 \times (1. - 0.33) = 9.84 \times 0.67$$
$$= 6.59\%$$

The investor would receive the same number of after-tax dollars from a taxable bond with a yield of 9.84% as he would from a tax-free bond with a yield of 6.59%

CALCULATOR GUIDE

▶ 9.84 M+ 1 − 0.33 × Mrc = ◀ **6.5928** or 6.59%

Note: Under current tax law there are relatively few different tax brackets. We are going to take a little license with the following self-test and ask questions using tax brackets that do not exist at present.

SELF-TEST

A. What is the taxable equivalent yield for a municipal bond yielding 5.90% for an investor in the 40% tax bracket?

B. What is the tax-exempt equivalent yield for an investor in the 55% tax bracket who is considering the purchase of a taxable bond yielding 8.86?

ANSWERS TO SELF-TEST

A. 9.83%   (5.90 ÷ (1. − 0.40) = 5.90 ÷ 0.6 = 9.83%)

▶ 1 − 0.40 M+ 5.90 ÷ Mrc = ◀ **9.8333333** or 9.83%

B. 3.99%   (8.86 × (1. − 0.55) = 3.99%)

▶ 8.86 M+ 1 − 0.55 × Mrc = ◀ **3.987** or 3.99%

Note the dramatic difference. For a person in tne 55% tax bracket, it only takes a tax-exempt yield of less than 4% to equal a taxable yield of 8.86%.

CHAPTER 13

PRICING TREASURY BILLS: DISCOUNT YIELDS, COUPON EQUIVALENT YIELDS

Discount Yields

T-bills are *discount instruments*. They do not have a coupon rate, and in fact do not pay any interest until they mature. EE savings bonds and zero-coupon bonds work the same way; such instruments are bought at a discount and the investor ultimately receives her interest when the security is redeemed, at par, when it matures. The difference between the discounted purchase price and par value represents the investor's interest.

T-bills are quoted to represent the discount at which they are trading. They have no "coupons" (no interest payments until maturity) and no stated rate of interest. They always trade at a discount from par since they can have no "reward" for holders beyond payment of par value at maturity.

It is true that some debt instruments trade at a premium for one of two reasons: They may be convertible, or they may have a coupon rate that is higher than newly issued instruments of similar quality. Neither of these conditions apply to T-bills because they are not convertible and do not have any coupon rate.

Therefore Treasury bills are quoted on a discounted yield basis, rather than on the yield-to-maturity method described in Chapter 9.

Example: A typical quote might be "5.31—5.29."

Such quotes are "in hundredths, on terms of a rate of discount"—or at least that's what it says in the fine print under the "Treasury Bonds, Notes & Bills" heading in the financial press.

Note that the bid yield is higher than the asked yield, for the very same reason as with other instruments quoted on a yield basis. The bid yield represents fewer dollars than the asked yield. (To review this concept, see Chapter 11.)

Converting a T-Bill Quote to Dollar Price

Here's the formula for converting a T-bill quote into dollars.

Step 1:

$$\text{Discount} = \text{Par Value} \times \frac{\text{Bid or Offer}}{\text{(in decimal form)}} \times \frac{\text{Days to Maturity}}{360}$$

Step 2:

$$\text{Dollar Price} = \text{Par Value} - \text{Discount}$$

Example: What is the dollar price for $100,000 T-bills maturing in 120 days that are offered at 5.89?

Step 1:

$$\text{Discount} = \text{Par Value} \times \frac{\text{Bid or Offer}}{\text{(in decimal form)}} \times \frac{\text{Days to Maturity}}{360}$$

$$= \$100,000 \times 0.0589 \times \frac{120}{360}$$

$$= \frac{\$706,800}{360}$$

$$= \$1,963.33$$

CALCULATOR GUIDE

▶ 100000 × 5.89 ÷ 100 × 120 ÷ 360 = ◀ **1963.3333**
                                         or $1,963.33

Step 2:

$$\text{Dollar Price} = \text{Par Value} - \text{Discount}$$
$$= \$100,000 - \$1,963.33 = \$98,036.67$$

Figure 13-1
Treasury Bill Quotes

Maturity	Days to Mat.	Bid	Asked	Chg.	Ask Yld.
Sep 19 '91	3	5.33	5.23	+ 0.01	5.32
Sep 26 '91	10	5.06	4.96	− 0.06	5.04
Oct 03 '91	17	5.03	4.93	− 0.07	5.02
Oct 10 '91	24	5.02	4.92	− 0.09	5.02
Oct 17 '91	31	5.03	4.99	− 0.07	5.10
Oct 24 '91	38	5.11	5.07	− 0.05	5.17
Oct 31 '91	45	5.13	5.09	− 0.05	5.21
Nov 07 '91	52	5.15	5.11	− 0.06	5.23
Nov 14 '91	59	5.17	5.15	− 0.05	5.28
Nov 21 '91	66	5.21	5.19	− 0.04	5.31
Nov 29 '91	74	5.20	5.18	− 0.04	5.32
Dec 05 '91	80	5.23	5.21	− 0.03	5.36
Dec 12 '91	87	5.22	5.20	− 0.04	5.35
Dec 19 '91	94	5.23	5.21	− 0.02	5.36
Dec 26 '91	101	5.20	5.18	− 0.04	5.34
Jan 02 '92	108	5.20	5.18	− 0.03	5.35
Jan 09 '92	115	5.23	5.21	− 0.04	5.39
Jan 16 '92	122	5.25	5.23	− 0.03	5.40
Jan 23 '92	129	5.25	5.23	− 0.03	5.42
Jan 30 '92	136	5.25	5.23	− 0.04	5.42
Feb 06 '92	143	5.26	5.24	− 0.03	5.44
Feb 13 '92	150	5.26	5.24	− 0.04	5.43
Feb 20 '92	157	5.26	5.24	− 0.03	5.45
Feb 27 '92	164	5.26	5.24	− 0.03	5.46
Mar 05 '92	171	5.26	5.24	− 0.03	5.46
Mar 12 '92	178	5.24	5.22	− 0.03	5.45
Apr 09 '92	206	5.24	5.22	− 0.04	5.45
Apr 23 '92	220	5.27	5.25	− 0.04	5.49
May 07 '92	234	5.27	5.25	− 0.04	5.49
Jun 04 '92	262	5.24	5.22	− 0.04	5.47
Jul 02 '92	290	5.27	5.25	− 0.04	5.52
Jul 30 '92	318	5.27	5.25	− 0.04	5.53
Aug 27 '92	346	5.25	5.23	− 0.04	5.53

(Courtesy of *The Wall Street Journal*, September 13, 1991.)

SELF-TEST

Use Figure 13-1 to answer the Self-Test questions.

A. What is the dollar value, using the asked price, for $50,000 par value of the Jan 02 '92 bills?

B. What is the amount of the "spread," in dollars, for $1,000,000 of the Apr 23 '92 bills? You will have to compare the dollar value for the block at the bid and at the offer price. The difference between the two values is the spread.

ANSWERS TO SELF-TEST

A. $49,223.00

Discount = $50,000 × 0.0518 × $\frac{108}{360}$ = $777.00

Dollar price = $50,000 − $777 = $49,223.00

▶ 50000 × 5.18 ÷ 100 × 108 ÷ 360 = ◀ **777.** or $777.00

▶ 50000 − 777 = ◀ **49223.** or $49,223.00

B. $122.20

The dollar price of the bid is $967,794.50 and the dollar price of the offer is $967,916.70. The difference between the two figures is only $122.20, typical of the very tight spreads in the T-bill market. The math works out this way:

Bid:

$1,000,000 × 0.0527 × $\frac{220}{360}$ = $32,205.56 discount

$1,000,000 − $32,205.56 = $967,794.50

(It's actually $967,794.44, but the calculator shows a very slightly different amount.)

▶ 1000000 × 5.27 ÷ 100 × 220 ÷ 360 = ◀ **32205.555,**
which rounds to 32205.56

▶ 1000000 − 32205.56 = ◀ **967794.5** or $967,794.50

Asked:

$1,000,000 × 0.0525 × $\frac{220}{360}$ = $32,083.33

$1,000,000 − $32,083.33 = $967,916.70

(Actually $967,916.67, but excuse the calculator.)

▶ 1000000 × 5.25 ÷ 100 × 220 ÷ 360 = ◀ **32083.333,**
which rounds to 32083.33

▶ 1000000 − 32083.33 = ◀ **967916.7** or $967,916.70

Spread:

$967,916.70 − $967,794.50 = $122.20

▶ 967916.70 − 967794.50 = ◀ **122.2** or $122.20

Note: These last questions were tough ones, probably well beyond anything they might test you on for series 7. You will certainly be asked to recognize a typical T-bill quote, but the important things to remember about T-bills are that they:

- Are the shortest-term government instruments.
- Have no stated rate of return (no coupons).
- Are not callable.
- Are "book entry" (not issued in physical form).
- Always trade at a discount and are quoted on a discount yield basis.

Coupon-Equivalent Yields

Examine Figure 13-1. In the right-hand column, "Ask Yld," you find the discount yield of the asked price as a "coupon-equivalent" yield. This column is included to make comparisons with other debt instruments more meaningful. It would be unfair to compare a discount yield with a "regular" bond yield since it would be misleading—"apples and oranges."

To convert a T-bill's discount yield to a coupon-equivalent yield, apply the following formula:

$$\text{Coupon-Equivalent Yield} = \frac{\text{Discount in Dollars}}{\text{Dollar Price}} \times \frac{365}{\text{Days to Maturity}}$$

Example: What is the coupon-equivalent yield for $100,000 of 120-day T-bills offered at a 6.26 discount yield? The first step is to work out the discount and the dollar price (as we did in the first part of this chapter):

$$\text{Discount} = \text{Par Value} \times \frac{\text{Bid or Offer}}{\text{(in decimal form)}} \times \frac{\text{Days to Maturity}}{360}$$

$$= \$100,000 \times 0.0626 \times \frac{120}{360}$$

$$= \$2,086.67$$

The second step is to calculate the dollar price:

$$\text{Dollar Price} = \text{Par Value} - \text{Discount}$$
$$= \$100,000 - \$2,086.67 = \$97,913.33$$

Now we have the numbers to substitute in the formula:

$$\text{Coupon-Equivalent Yield} = \frac{\text{Discount in Dollars}}{\text{Dollar Price}} \times \frac{365}{\text{Days to Maturity}}$$

$$= \frac{\$2,086.67}{\$97,913.33} \times \frac{365}{120} = 6.48\%$$

Note: The coupon-equivalent yield will always be higher than the discount yield.

There will be no Self-Test on this formula since it is well beyond the scope of the series 7 exam.

CHAPTER 14

PRICING MUTUAL FUNDS

Mutual funds, also known as open-end investment companies, are one of the few securities products priced in dollars and cents. A typical quote for a loaded fund (i.e., a fund with a sales charge) might read "8.80—9.36." This fund quoted has a bid of $8.80 and an offer price of $9.36 per share. As we will see in the next chapter, these are not the typical "highest bid and lowest offer" quotations established in the open market.

- A mutual fund's *bid* is, in effect, its liquidating value; it is its net asset value per share, what you would receive if you *sell* a share of the fund.

- The *offer* price is the bid plus the sales charge, if any, or what it costs to *buy* a share of the fund.

A no-load fund (i.e., a fund without a sales charge) might be "12.45—NL." This fund has a bid *and* an offer price of $12.45 per share, because there is no sales charge.

To establish the total market value of any mutual fund shares held, multiply the number of shares owned by the fund's bid price.

Total Market Value = Number of Shares × Bid Price

Example: What is the total market value of a holding of 453 shares of a mutual fund quoted at 21.08—23.04?

Total Market Value = Number of Shares × Bid Price
= 453 × $21.08 = $9,549.24

Note: You multiply by the *bid* price because ordinarily that is the price you receive when you redeem mutual fund shares. Certain funds charge a redemption fee and, if so, the actual liquidating value will be lower than arrived at in the formula.

CALCULATOR GUIDE

▶ 453 × 21.08 = ◀ **9549.24** or $9,549.24

SELF-TEST

Use Figure 14-1 to answer the Self-Test questions.

A. A client owns two funds under the Shearson Funds group, 257.337 shares of ATG fund, and 579.571 shares of AZ Mu fund. What is the total market value of her holdings?

B. What would be the cost of 1,500 shares of Inco fund, a member of the Strong Funds group?

Figure 14-1
Mutual Fund Quotations

	NAV	Offer NAV Price	Chg.		NAV	Offer NAV Price	Chg.
Shearson Funds:				StratDv	25.87	NL	−.01
Advsr p	22.46	23.77	+.13	Strat Gth	19.46	NL	+.05
AgrGr	20.97	22.07	+.40	**Strong Funds:**			
Aprec	9.74	10.25	+.02	Advtg	9.79	NL	...
ATG	8.31	8.75	+.08	CmStk	13.61	13.89	+.06
ATIn	123.61	123.61	−.28	Discov	18.43	18.81	+.16
AZ Mu	9.73	10.24	+.02	GovSc	10.44	NL	+.01
CalMu	15.97	16.81	+.03	Inco	9.24	NL	+.01
FdVal	6.47	6.81	...	Invst	19.08	19.27	+.04
GlbOp	25.13	26.45	+.01	MunBd	9.54	NL	+.01
HiYld	12.55	13.21	+.01	Oppty	20.15	20.56	+.08
MgdG	12.45	13.11	+.02	ST Bd	9.81	NL	...
MMun	15.43	16.24	+.03	Total	18.79	18.98	+.10
MAMu	12.23	12.87	+.02	**SunAmerica Fds:**			
NJMu	12.53	13.19	+.02	AgGth p	13.86	14.71	+.13
NYMu	16.50	17.37	+.02	BalAs f	16.89	16.89	+.07
1990s p	9.80	10.32	+.18	CapAp t	11.66	11.66	+.11
PrcM	12.79	13.46	−.04	CvSec p	9.58	10.06	+.01
PrnRt	11.26	NL	−.01	EmGr t	15.04	15.04	+.10
PrInII	8.32	NL	+.01	Glbln t	9.88	9.88	...
PrInIII	7.73	NL	+.05	Grwth p	13.98	14.83	+.14
SmCa	17.84	18.78	+.40	HInc t	7.29	7.29	−.01
Winc p	7.57	7.80	...	HiYld p	8.57	9.00	+.01
WWPr p	1.96	1.96	...	Home t	10.63	10.63	+.01
Shearson Ports:				IncPl t	6.91	6.91	+.01
Convt t	12.96	12.96	+.03	Stripe p	12.40	13.02	...
DirVal t	14.01	14.01	+.10	TotRt p	13.59	14.42	+.06
DvsInc	8.19	8.19	+.01	GvSc p	9.90	10.39	+.01
Europ t	13.13	13.13	+.04	USGv t	8.94	8.94	...
GlbBd t	15.55	15.55	+.04	**TNE Funds:**			
GlbEq t	10.76	10.76	+.01	Balan p	9.56	10.22	−.01
GvSec t	9.39	9.39	+.01	BdInc p	11.54	12.08	+.01

(Courtesy of *The Wall Street Journal,* September 23, 1991.)

ANSWERS TO SELF-TEST

A. $7,777.70

ATG fund	257.337 × $8.31 =	$2,138.47
Az Mu fund	579.571 × $9.73 =	$5,639.23
		$7,777.70

We multiply by the bid prices to figure total value. The bid price is what the holder would receive if she liquidates. Note the fractional shares of each holding. Mutual funds can be bought to three decimal places (thousandths of a share), as in our example, and sometimes even to four decimal places (ten-thousandths of a share).

▶ 257.337 × 8.31 M+ 579.571 × 9.73 M+ Mrc

                      = ◀ **7777.6962** or $7,777.70

B. $13,860.00   (1500 × 9.24 = $13,860.00)

This is a no-load fund. Its bid and asked prices are the same, $9.24.

▶ 1500 × 9.24 = ◀ **13860.** or $13,860.00

CHAPTER 15

MUTUAL FUNDS

Net Asset Value

A mutual fund's *net asset value* (its "bid") is the actual underlying value of a single share of the fund. In theory, if the entire fund were to be liquidated—if all the assets were sold and all the liabilities paid off—the net asset value per share is the dollar amount that would be distributed to each share of the fund.

Each fund figures its net asset value (its "bid") at least once every business day. This requires that they first establish a fair market value for every one of their *assets*—all their stocks, bonds, cash, money market instruments, and other holdings, all their accumulated interest, all dividends due (past the ex-dividend date but before the payment date), and any other assets. Then they must account for all their *liabilities*. The difference between the total assets and the total liabilities is the fund's *net assets*. Dividing this figure by the number of fund shares outstanding gives the net asset value per share. This computation can be summarized as follows:

$$\text{Net Asset Value per Share} = \frac{\text{Total Assets} - \text{Total Liabilities}}{\text{Number of Shares Outstanding}}$$

Note: Net asset value changes as the value of the fund's portfolio goes up and down. Purchases and sales of the fund itself, however, do *not* affect the net asset value.

SELF-TEST

A. XYZ mutual fund has 2,500,000 shares outstanding. It has total assets of $28,000,000 and total liabilities of $5,000,000. What is XYZ Fund's net asset value (NAV) per share?

B. What dollar amount would be received by an investor liquidating 1,750.314 shares of XYZ Fund?

ANSWERS TO SELF-TEST

A. $9.20   ($28,000,000 − 5,000,000 ÷ 2,500,000 = $9.20)

▶ 28000000 − 5000000 ÷ 2500000 = ◀ **9.2** or $9.20

B. $16,102.98   (1,750.314 × $9.20 = 16,102.89)

▶ 1750.314 × 9.20 = ◀ **16102.888** or $16,102.89

Offering Price

A mutual fund's *offering price* (asked price) can range anywhere from the bid price (NAV) to approximately 9.3% more than the bid. The "cheapest" price for a mutual fund, for example, with a $10.00 net asset value would be $10.00 per share. This would represent a no-load fund. It would be quoted either as "10.00—10.00" or "10.00—NL." (The letters "NL" stand for "no load.")

Example: In Figure 15-1, note the first three funds in the right-hand column. These are no-load funds, which do not charge a commission on purchases. They levy no sales charges. These funds are both bought and sold (redeemed) at their bid prices, or NAVs.

At the other end of the scale is the loaded fund, whose asked price consists of the bid plus the sales charge, or "load."

Example: A fund's bid-asked prices are quoted as 10.00—10.93. The difference between the bid and asked, $0.93, is the sales charge. If you compute this sales charge as a percent of the bid, it represents a 9.3% fee ($0.93 ÷ $10.00 = 9.3%). Computed as a percent of the asked price, the fee works out to 8.5% ($0.93 ÷ $10.93 = 8.5%).

Figure 15-1
Mutual Fund Quotations

	NAV	Offer NAV Price	Chg.		NAV	Offer NAV Price	Chg.
Shearson Funds:				StratDv	25.87	NL	−.01
Advsr p	22.46	23.77	+.13	Strat Gth	19.46	NL	+.05
AgrGr	20.97	22.07	+.40	**Strong Funds:**			
Aprec	9.74	10.25	+.02	Advtg	9.79	NL	...
ATG	8.31	8.75	+.08	CmStk	13.61	13.89	+.06
ATIn	123.61	123.61	−.28	Discov	18.43	18.81	+.16
AZ Mu	9.73	10.24	+.02	GovSc	10.44	NL	+.01
CalMu	15.97	16.81	+.03	Inco	9.24	NL	+.01
FdVal	6.47	6.81	...	Invst	19.08	19.27	+.04
GlbOp	25.13	26.45	+.01	MunBd	9.54	NL	+.01
HiYld	12.55	13.21	+.01	Oppty	20.15	20.56	+.08
MgdG	12.45	13.11	+.02	ST Bd	9.81	NL	...
MMun	15.43	16.24	+.03	Total	18.79	18.98	+.10
MAMu	12.23	12.87	+.02	**SunAmerica Fds:**			
NJMu	12.53	13.19	+.02	AgGth p	13.86	14.71	+.13
NYMu	16.50	17.37	+.02	BalAs f	16.89	16.89	+.07
1990s p	9.80	10.32	+.18	CapAp t	11.66	11.66	+.11
PrcM	12.79	13.46	−.04	CvSec p	9.58	10.06	+.01
PrnRt	11.26	NL	−.01	EmGr t	15.04	15.04	+.10
PrnII	8.32	NL	+.01	GlbIn t	9.88	9.88	...
PrnIII	7.73	NL	+.05	Grwth p	13.98	14.83	+.14
SmCa	17.84	18.78	+.40	HIinc t	7.29	7.29	−.01
WInc p	7.57	7.80	...	HiYld p	8.57	9.00	+.01
WWPr p	1.96	1.96	...	Home t	10.63	10.63	+.01
Shearson Ports:				IncPI t	6.91	6.91	+.01
Convt t	12.96	12.96	+.03	Stripe p	12.40	13.02	...
DirVal t	14.01	14.01	+.10	TotRt p	13.59	14.42	+.06
DvsInc	8.19	8.19	+.01	GvSc p	9.90	10.39	+.01
Europ t	13.13	13.13	+.04	USGv t	8.94	8.94	...
GlbBd t	15.55	15.55	+.04	**TNE Funds:**			
GlbEq t	10.76	10.76	+.01	Balan p	9.56	10.22	−.01
GvSec t	9.39	9.39	+.01	BdInc p	11.54	12.08	+.01
GrOpr t	16.80	16.80	+.08	GlobG p	11.86	12.42	...

(Courtesy of *The Wall Street Journal,* September 23, 1991.)

That's the legal maximum for a noncontractual plan purchase, 8.5% figured as a percent of the fund's offering price. Many funds are no-load, and many of the load funds levy a sales charge much below the legal maximum.

Here's how loaded funds figure their asked (offering) prices:

$$\text{Offer Price} = \frac{\text{Net Asset Value}}{1. - \text{Percent Sales Charge}}$$

Example: A mutual fund has a net asset value of $18.87 and levies a 7% sales charge figured as a percent of the offer price. What is the fund's offer price?

$$\text{Offer Price} = \frac{\text{Net Asset Value}}{1. - \text{Percent Sales Charge}}$$

$$= \frac{\$18.87}{1. - 0.07} = \frac{\$18.87}{0.93} = \$20.29$$

CALCULATOR GUIDE

▶ 100 − 7 ÷ 100 M+ 18.87 ÷ Mrc = ◀ **20.290322**
                                                              or $20.29

Newspaper listings for loaded funds show the offering (asked) price reflecting the *highest* sales charge levied by that fund. Sometimes the customer is entitled to buy at a sales charge less than the maximum such as when buying at a "breakpoint" or under rights of accumulation (both methods described later in this chapter). In such cases, the appropriate offer price must be recalculated.

Example: The fund in the previous example charges only 5% for large purchases. In such cases the offer price would be $19.86 rather than $20.29. At 5% the calculation would be:

$$\text{Offer Price} = \frac{\text{Net Asset Value}}{1. - \text{Percent Sales Charge}}$$

$$= \frac{\$18.87}{1. - 0.05} = \frac{\$18.87}{0.95} = \$19.86$$

CALCULATOR GUIDE

▶ 100 − 5 ÷ 100 M+ 18.87 ÷ Mrc = ◀ **19.863157**
                                                              or $19.86

SELF-TEST

A. Maria Fund has a net asset value of $21.24 per share and charges an 8½% sales fee. What is the fund's offering price?

B. The sales charge on the fund described in question A is reduced to 7% for purchases between $10,000 and $24,999. What would be the offer price for a $15,000 purchase?

ANSWERS TO SELF-TEST

A. $23.21   (21.24 ÷ (1. − 0.085) = 21.24 ÷ 0.915 = $23.21)

▶ 100 − 8.5 ÷ 100 M+ 21.24 ÷ Mrc = ◀ **23.213114**
                                                              or $23.21

B. $22.84   (21.24 ÷ (1. − 0.07) = 21.24 ÷ 0.93 = $22.84)

▶ 100 − 7 ÷ 100 M+ 21.24 ÷ Mrc = ◀ **22.838709**
                                                              or $22.84

Note: The client is not charged 8½% for the first $10,000 worth of the purchase and 7% on the last $5,000. The lesser sales charge (7%) is charged on the entire purchase.

Sales Charges

Sales charges range from zero (no-load funds) to a maximum of 8½% of the offering price (9% for contractual plans). Newspaper listings show a fund's maximum sales charge. It is possible to deduce a fund's maximum sales charge percentage from its newspaper listing by dividing the fund's load (the difference between the bid and the asked price) by its asked price.

$$\text{Maximum Sales Charge} = \frac{\text{Offer Price} - \text{Bid Price}}{\text{Offer Price}}$$

Example: A mutual fund is quoted 14.25—15.49. What is the fund's maximum sales charge, expressed as a percent of the offering price?

$$\text{Maximum Sales Charge} = \frac{\text{Offer Price} - \text{Bid Price}}{\text{Offer Price}}$$

$$= \frac{15.49 - 14.25}{15.49} = \frac{1.24}{15.49} = 8.0\%$$

CALCULATOR GUIDE

▶ 15.49 − 14.25 ÷ 15.49 × 100 = ◀ **8.00516** or 8.0%

Note: The sales charge may be figured as a percent of the bid or as a percent of the offer price. Figured as a percent of the bid, it will be higher than when figured as a percent of the asked price. A mutual fund's prospectus shows both methods of figuration, but salespersons are permitted to use either method. They usually choose the "percent of offer price" approach, and this is known as the "usual" industry method. You should also use this method when taking the series 6 or series 7 examinations. When in doubt, use this same method (percent of offer price).

SELF-TEST

A. What is the percent sales charge for a mutual fund quoted 9.94—10.69?

B. What is the percent sales charge for a mutual fund quoted 9.15—10.00?

C. Refer to Figure 15-1. What is the percent sales charge for Shearson's NJ Mu fund?

ANSWERS TO SELF-TEST

A. 7.0%   (10.69 − 9.94 ÷ 10.69 = 7.0%)

▶ 10.69 − 9.94 ÷ 10.69 × 100 = ◀ **7.0159** or 7.0%

B. 8.5%   (10.00 − 9.15 ÷ 10.00 = 8.5%)

▶ 10.00 − 9.15 ÷ 10.00 × 100 = ◀ **8.5** or 8.5%

C. 5.0%   (13.19 − 12.53 ÷ 13.19 = 5.0%)

▶ 13.19 − 12.53 ÷ 13.19 × 100 = ◀ **5.00379** or 5.0%

Redemption Fees

Some funds charge a *redemption fee*, which is a fee that is subtracted from the amount received by a person redeeming at full net asset value. It may be small, such as a fraction of 1%, or relatively significant. Redemption fees are usually limited to no-load or low-load funds, while other funds levy a "contingent deferred sales charge." This is, in effect, a "back-end" load. If a shareholder redeems fund shares relatively soon after purchasing them, the deferred sales charge is high but becomes progressively lower over time. There may be no redemption fee at all for shares held for a relatively long time.

$$\text{Redemption Value} = (\text{Number of Shares} \times \text{NAV})$$
$$\times (1 - \% \text{ Redemption Fee})$$

Example: What would be the proceeds of the redemption of 1,443 shares of a fund with a net asset value (NAV) of $21.47 and a redemption fee of 2%?

$$\text{Redemption Value} = (\text{Number of Shares} \times \text{NAV})$$
$$\times (1 - \% \text{ Redemption Fee})$$
$$= (1443 \times \$21.47) \times (1 - 0.02)$$
$$= 30,981.21 \times 0.98 = \$30,361.59$$

CALCULATOR GUIDE

▶ 1443 × 21.47 M+ 100 − 2 ÷ 100 × Mrc = ◀ **30361.585**
or $30,361.59

SELF-TEST

A. What would be the proceeds of the redemption of 1,200 shares of a fund with a net asset value of $14.88 and a redemption fee of 3/4 of 1%?

B. A mutual fund charges a redemption fee of 2.5% It is quoted at $19.66—$20.48. How much money would a client receive after redeeming 12,250 shares?

ANSWERS TO SELF-TEST

A. $17,722.08   [(1200 × $14.88) × (1. − 0.0075) = $17,722.08]

3/4 of 1%, in decimal format, is 0.0075

▶ 1200 × 14.88 M+ 100 − 0.75 ÷ 100 × Mrc

= ◀ **17722.08** or $17,722.08

B. $234,814.12   [(12,250 × $19.66 × (1. − 0.025) = $234,814.12]

Remember to use the bid price when calculating redemption. The offer price is what the fund costs to *buy*.

▶ 12250 × 19.66   M+ 100 − 2.5 ÷ 100 × Mrc

= ◀ **234814.12** or 234,814.12

Breakpoint Sales

Most loaded funds offer reduced sales charges for bulk purchases. The discounted sales charges vary widely, as do the amounts you have to purchase to receive these reduced charges.

Example: Figure 15-2 shows a "breakpoint" chart that is fairly typical for the mutual fund industry. The chart shows that the purchase price will vary with the dollar amount invested. Purchases of the fund in any dollar amount less than $10,000 will incur a sales charge of 8.50%. Purchases of $10,000 to $24,999 will be charged only 7.75%. The sales charges are further reduced as detailed in the chart.

Assume that Marobeth fund has a net asset value of $26.82 per share. A $5,000 purchase would be charged 8.50% The offer price for such a purchase would be figured as explained in the "Offering Price" section earlier in this chapter.

Figure 15-2
A Typical Breakpoint Chart

Amount of Purchase	Sales Charge (as a percent of offering price)
Less than $10,000	8.50%
$10,000 to $24,999	7.75%
$25,000 to $49,999	6.00%
$50,000 to $99,999	4.50%
$100,000 to $249,999	3.50%
$250,000 to $399,999	2.50%
$400,000 to $599,999	2.00%
$600,000 to $4,999,999	1.00%
$5,000,000 or more	0.25%

$$\text{Offer Price} = \frac{\text{Net Asset Value}}{1. - \text{Percent Sales Charge}}$$

$$= \frac{\$28.62}{1. - 0.085} = \frac{\$28.62}{0.915} = \$31.28$$

CALCULATOR GUIDE

▶ 100 − 8.5 ÷ 100 M+   28.62 ÷ Mrc = ◀ **31.278688**

or $31.28

Example: Figure the offering price for a $60,000 purchase of the Marobeth fund in the previous example:

$$\text{Offer Price} = \frac{\text{Net Asset Value}}{1. - \text{Percent Sales Charge}}$$

$$= \frac{\$28.62}{1. - 0.045} = \frac{\$28.62}{0.955} = \$29.97$$

CALCULATOR GUIDE

▶ 100 − 4.5 ÷ 100 M+   28.62 ÷ Mrc = ◀ **29.968586**

or $29.97

The $5,000 share purchase would be effected at an offering price of $31.28 (8.5% sales charge), and the investor would receive 159.847 shares: $5,000 ÷ 31.28 = 159.847. A purchase of $60,000 would be made at an offer price of $29.97 (4.5% sales charge), and the investor would receive 2002.002 shares: $60,000 ÷ 29.97 = 2002.002.

SELF-TEST

Use the breakpoint chart in Figure 15-2 to answer the questions.

A. Given a NAV of $24.50, what would be the offer price used for a purchase of $12,000 worth of Marobeth Fund?

B. How many shares would the customer receive (refer to previous question)?

ANSWERS TO SELF-TEST

A. $26.56

$$\frac{\$24.50}{1. - 0.0775} = \frac{\$24.50}{0.9225} = \$26.56$$

Using the chart, a $12,000 purchase falls within the "$10,000 to $24,999" bracket, which calls for a 7.75% sales charge.

▶ 100 − 7.75 ÷ 100 M+ 24.50 ÷ Mrc = ◀ **26.558265**
or $26.56

B. 451.807 shares (12,000 26.56 = 451.807)

▶ 12000 ÷ 26.56 = ◀ **451.80722** or 451.807 shares

Right of Accumulation

Many mutual funds permit additional purchases in voluntary (open) accounts at the breakpoint appropriate to the total of the shareholder's *previous* purchases plus the current purchase. The offer price formula is adjusted to reflect the right of accumulation:

$$\text{Offer Price} = \frac{\text{Net Asset Value}}{1. - (\text{Percent Sales Charge} + \text{Old Holdings})}$$

Example: Refer to the breakpoint chart in Figure 15-2. Mr. Cartlidge has bought shares of Marobeth Fund over the past several years and owns a total of $49,250 worth of the fund. If he now makes an additional purchase of $5,000, he will only be required to pay a sales charge of 4.50% because the value of his "old" shares ($49,250), added to the value of the shares he is now purchasing ($5,000), puts the new purchase in the "$50,000 to $99,999" bracket. It is too late to adjust the sales charge on the previous purchases since they were effected over a number of years, but the new purchase qualifies for the reduced sales charge. Assume that the current bid (NAV) is $26.46.

$$\text{Offer Price} = \frac{\text{Net Asset Value}}{1. - (\text{Percent Sales Charge} + \text{Old Holdings})}$$

$$= \frac{\$26.46}{1. - 0.045} = \frac{\$26.46}{0.955} = \$27.71$$

Mr. Cartlidge will be able to make his new purchase ($5,000 worth) at the offering price that would normally apply to a purchase of $50,000 to $99,999. Note that the reduced sales charge applies to the entire new purchase, not just to the amount in excess of a total holding of $50,000.

CALCULATOR GUIDE

▶ 100 − 4.5 ÷ 100 M+ 26.46 ÷ Mrc = ◀ **27.706806**
                                          or $27.71

SELF-TEST

Use Figure 15-2 to answer the following questions. Assume a current bid price for the fund of $20.38.

A. James Treanor owns $9,000 worth of Marobeth Fund—figured at the offering price—that he has bought over the past several years. He now wishes to make an additional investment of $3,000 in the fund. At what offering price will his new purchase be effected?

B. How many shares will Mr. Treanor receive from this new purchase? Figure your answer to 3 decimal places.

ANSWERS TO SELF-TEST

A. $22.09

$$\frac{\$20.38}{1. - 0.0775} = \frac{\$20.38}{0.9225} = \$22.09$$

He will buy at the 7.75% sales charge because his "old" holdings ($9,000) and his new purchase ($3,000) will put his total holdings in the $10,000 to $24,999 bracket.

▶ 100 − 7.75 ÷ 100 M+ 20.38 ÷ Mrc = ◀ **22.09214**
                                          or $22.09

B. 226.347 shares   ($5,000 ÷ 22.09 = 226.347)

▶ 5000 ÷ 22.09 = ◀ **226.34676** or 226.347 shares

CHAPTER 16

RIGHTS OFFERINGS

During a rights offering, the rights to subscribe for the "new" stock are distributed to the "old" shareholders, usually on a one-right-per-old-share basis. The number of rights needed to subscribe to a new share is established by the ratio of old shares to new shares.

Rights to Subscribe = Shares Outstanding ÷ New Shares

Example: If a company with 1,000,000 old shares outstanding wishes to issue 200,000 shares of new stock, it will require 5 rights to subscribe for 1 new share. If there are 1,000,000 old shares to start with and each share receives one right, then the 1,000,000 rights issued will be used to subscribe for the 200,000 new shares.

Rights to Subscribe = Shares Outstanding ÷ New Shares
= 1,000,000 ÷ 200,000
= 5 rights to subscribe to 1 new share

Theoretical Value

There should be some direct relationship between the market price of the rights and their actual value. If the rights are selling at the "right" price, they are said to be trading at their *theoretical value*. There are two formulas for determining a right's theoretical value:

- One is used when the old stock is trading cum (with) rights. During the cum-rights period, a purchaser receives

one right, together with each of the old shares he purchases.

● One is used when the old stock is trading ex (without)
rights. During the old stock's ex-rights period, a purchaser
will receive only stock.

Old Stock Trading Ex-Rights

When the old stock is trading ex-rights, the following formula is used:

$$\text{Theoretical Value of a Right} = \frac{\text{Market Price} - \text{Subscription Price}}{\text{Number of Rights Needed to Subscribe}}$$

Example: What is the theoretical value of a right in an
offering under the following circumstances?

● The old stock is trading at $40 per share (ex-rights).

● The subscription price at $38.

● It takes 4 rights to subscribe to 1 new share.

$$\text{Theoretical Value of a Right} = \frac{\text{Market Price} - \text{Subscription Price}}{\text{Number of Rights Needed to Subscribe}}$$

$$= \frac{\$40 - \$38}{4} = \frac{\$2}{4} = \$0.50$$

CALCULATOR GUIDE

▶ 40 − 38 ÷ 4 = ◀ **0.5** or **$0.50**

You can check to see if the theoretical value you arrive at
is accurate. After you figure the theoretical value of a right,
compare the cost of buying the stock outright with the cost of
buying rights at their theoretical value and then subscribing
for the shares. You should arrive at an identical cost using
either method. If the rights are trading at their theoretical
value (commission costs not included), you should pay exactly the same for an outright stock purchase as you would for
first buying rights and then subscribing.

Example: Let's check our answer in the previous example by
comparing the costs of buying old stock versus buying 4
rights and subscribing to stock.

Buying stock outright would cost $40:

- Buying the 4 rights necessary to subscribe for a share, at their theoretical value of $0.50 each (that's the figure we arrived at in our example) comes to $2 (4 × $0.50).
- Subscribing costs $38.

The total cost is $40 ($2 + $38), which is the price at which the old stock is trading. The numbers check out!

Old Stock Trading Cum-Rights

You must add 1 to the denominator when figuring rights value during the period that the old stock is trading cum-rights. The formula becomes:

$$\frac{\text{Theoretical Value}}{\text{of a Right}} = \frac{\text{Market Price} - \text{Subscription Price}}{1 + \text{Number of Rights Needed to Subscribe}}$$

Example: What is the theoretical value of a right in the following offering?

- The old stock is trading at 58½ (cum-rights).
- The subscription price is 54⅞.
- It requires 7 rights to subscribe for 1 new share.

$$\frac{\text{Theoretical Value}}{\text{of a Right}} = \frac{\text{Market Price} - \text{Subscription Price}}{1 + \text{Number of Rights Needed to Subscribe}}$$
$$= \frac{\$58.50 - \$54.875}{1 + 7} = \frac{\$3.625}{8} = \$0.453$$

This is slightly more than $0.45.

CALCULATOR GUIDE

▶ 1 + 7 M+ 58.5 − 54.875 ÷ Mrc = ◀ **0.453125**
                                              or $0.45

Let's again check our answer by comparing the outright purchase cost with the "buy rights and subscribe" cost.

Example: Buying a share of stock outright would cost $58.50, but, since the stock is trading cum-rights, you get a right with the stock. You, of course, can immediately sell this right at its theoretical value of $0.45, reducing your overall cost to just $58.05 ($58.50 − $0.45 = $58.05).

If you *subscribed* to a share by buying the required 7 rights at $0.45 each and paying the subscription price of

$54.875, you would be spending the same amount as for the
outright purchase of a share (7 × $0.45 + $54.875 =
$58.03)! (The 2-cent difference is accounted for because we
didn't use the right's value to those ''extra'' decimal places.)

CHAPTER 17

CONVERTIBLE SECURITIES

Some preferred stocks and corporate bonds are convertible into other securities, usually the common stock of the company issuing the fixed-income security. Those considering the purchase of a convertible security should know how many shares of common stock they will receive if and when they convert. The literature available to the financial professional describes the convertibility feature as a conversion *price*. The financial professional translates the conversion price into the conversion *ratio*, which is much more easily understood by the investing public.

Conversion Price

The *conversion price* of a convertible preferred stock or corporate bond is the price at which the security may be converted into another security. The price might be expressed as "convertible at 50" or "convertible @ $50." Sometimes the word "at" is used, sometimes the symbol (@) is used. The literature sometimes lists the conversion price with a dollar sign ($), sometimes without one.

Example: The following expressions all mean precisely the same thing:

  convertible at $25
  convertible @ $25
  convertible at 25
  convertible @ 25

The $25 figure is the conversion price.

The conversion price, which is the figure that practicing financial professionals use, is set by the company issuing the convertible security when it is first issued.

Conversion Ratio: Stocks

In order to be more meaningful to the investing public, the conversion price is restated as the conversion ratio. The *conversion ratio* is the number of shares of common stock that will be received by an investor in exchange for his/her convertible security. This is much easier to understand for investors who are contemplating the purchase of a convertible security. They want to know how many shares of common stock they will be entitled to if and when they convert. To compute a convertible instrument's conversion ratio, divide its par value by the conversion price. This gives the actual number of shares of common stock that will be received upon conversion.

$$\text{Conversion Ratio} = \frac{\text{Convertible Security's Par Value}}{\text{Conversion Price}}$$

Example: What is the conversion ratio for a convertible preferred stock (par value $100) that is convertible at 50?

$$\text{Conversion Ratio} = \frac{\text{Convertible Security's Par Value}}{\text{Conversion Price}}$$
$$= \frac{\$100}{50} = 2$$

The conversion ratio is 2. An investor who converts will receive 2 shares of common stock in exchange for 1 share of the convertible preferred.

CALCULATOR GUIDE
▶ 100 ÷ 50 = ◀ **2.** The conversion ratio is 2.

Don't assume that all preferred stocks have a par value of $100. While $100 is fairly common, there are many others.

Example: If the preferred stock in the previous example had a par value of $50, its conversion ratio would have been only 1 (50 ÷ 50)! It's easier with convertible bonds since you are always dealing with a par value of $1,000.

SELF-TEST

A. What is the conversion ratio for a $37.50 par value preferred stock convertible at 20?

B. How many shares of common stock will be received in exchange for a convertible debenture convertible at $48.97?

ANSWERS TO SELF-TEST

A. 1.875   ($37.50 ÷ 20 = 1.875 shares)

▶ 37.50 ÷ 20 = ◀ **1.875** or 1.875 shares

B. 20.42   ($1,000 ÷ 48.97 = 20.42 shares)

▶ 1000 ÷ 48.97 = ◀ **20.420665** or 20.42 shares

Note: When figuring the conversion ratio for a convertible bond, always use $1,000 as the par value.

Parity

When a convertible security and its underlying common stock are trading at "balanced" prices, they are said to be *at parity*. This means that the package of common stock receivable upon conversion and the convertible security are selling for equal dollar amounts.

Example: A convertible bond is trading at 120 ($1,200) and the underlying common stock is trading at 60. The bond is convertible @ 50.

First change the conversion price to the conversion ratio (it's a lot easier to work with) by dividing the convertible's par value by the conversion price:

$$\text{Conversion Ratio} = \frac{\text{Convertible Security's Par Value}}{\text{Conversion Price}}$$

$$= \frac{\$1,000}{50} = 20$$

The bond is trading for $1,200, but its par value is $1,000. You have now changed the conversion price of 50 to a conversion ratio of 20. This means that the bond can be converted into 20 shares of common stock. The bond is trading at parity with the common stock if and when its price and the total price of the 20 shares of common stock into which it is convertible are the same.

Let's compare the price of the bond and the value of the shares into which it is convertible:

Convertible
Security's Price = Conversion Ratio × Price per Share
            = 20 × 60 = $1,200

The securities are at parity. This is demonstrated by the fact that the price of the convertible bond ($1,200) and the value of the 20 shares of common stock into which it is convertible (20 × $60 = $1,200) are the same.

SELF-TEST

A. A convertible bond has a conversion ratio of 32. The common stock into which it is convertible is trading at 35⅝. What is parity for the convertible bond?

B. A convertible preferred stock ($50 par) has a conversion price of 20 and is trading at 107¼. The common stock into which it is convertible is trading at 41½. Is the preferred stock trading at, above, or below parity?

ANSWERS TO SELF-TEST

A. $1,140   (114)
  The question gave you the conversion ratio, which indicates that the bond can be exchanged for (converted into) 32 shares of common stock. A parity price for the bond would be the total value of the 32 shares of stock, or $1,140 (32 × 35⅝). If the bond is trading at parity with the common stock, it would be quoted at 114, which translates to $1,140.

B. Above parity
  The first step is to find parity and then to compare it with the actual trading price of the convertible stock. The conversion ratio must be found by dividing the preferred stock's par value by the conversion price.

$$\$50 \div 20 = 2.5$$

That's the conversion ratio—2.5 shares of common will be received for every share of convertible preferred exchanged. Therefore, the preferred would be considered to be trading at parity if and when its price is equal to the value of 2.5 shares of the common stock it may be exchanged for.

A parity price for the preferred would be equal to the conversion ratio multiplied by the price of the common stock.

$$2.5 \times 41\frac{1}{2} = 103\frac{3}{4}$$

A price of 103¾ would be parity for the preferred. The question stated that the preferred was trading at 107¼ which is 3½ points above parity.

Arbitrage

When the prices of a convertible instrument and the underlying common stock are not in balance, a "riskless arbitrage" situation may exist. Such opportunities are fleeting and can usually be exploited only by the professionals specializing in such activities (arbitrageurs). The following example is exaggerated but illustrative.

Example: A convertible preferred is trading at parity with its underlying common stock. The preferred may be exchanged for 2 shares of common. It is selling for 57, exactly 2 times the price of the common stock, which is trading at 28½. The preferred stock is at parity.

If a flood of buy orders pushes the price of the common stock up dramatically, say to 31, quick-thinking arbitrageurs would buy all the convertible preferred shares they could at any prices up to 62. Let's assume that they buy a total of 3,000 shares of the convertible preferred at various prices between 57 and 62, with an average price of 60 for the preferred shares purchased. They then issue instructions to convert the preferred stock to common stock and immediately sell 6,000 shares of the common stock at 31. Thus—by converting the 3,000 preferred they purchased—they get the 6,000 shares of common to sell.

Here's the arithmetic:

- They purchase 3,000 shares of preferred at an average price of 60 per share for a total purchase price of $180,000 ($3,000 × 60).

- They sell 6,000 shares of common stock at 31 per share for a total sale price of $186,000 (6,000 × 31).

Buying for $180,000 and simultaneously selling for $186,000 nets a profit of $6,000. That's an arbitrage! Now that the arbitrageurs have pushed the price of the convertible up to 62 with their buying, the preferred is selling at parity with the common stock and the arbitrage opportunity no longer exists.

"Forced" Conversion

Most convertible instruments are callable. When the issue is called, the holder has been put on notice that she has only a short time to "switch" the convertible stock or bond into common stock before the convertible instrument will be retired. She can either convert during this time, or accept the call and give up her convertible security for the call money the company is offering.

When the call goes out, holders must decide whether it is in their best interest to accept the call or to convert. If they do not convert, receiving common stock in exchange, they will receive cash. Sometimes it is better to accept the call; sometimes it is more advantageous to convert to common stock.

Example: Joan Bradley owns XYZ convertible preferred stock, $100 par, and is notified that her stock will be called at 102½ in one month. The conversion price is $20, and the common stock is trading at 14¾. The convertible preferred is trading at 75. Should Joan accept the call or convert?

If she converts, she will receive 5 shares of common stock ($100 par value ÷ 20 conversion price) trading at 14¾, which would give her a total value of $73.75 (5 × 14.75). If she does not convert and simply accepts the call at $102.50, she will be better off than converting to $73.75 worth of common stock. Her best course, obviously, would be to accept the call.

Example: Steve Rizek owns a convertible bond, convertible at $55, which is trading at 112¼. The underlying common stock is trading at 60½ when the bond is called at 101½. Should Steve accept the call or convert?

If Steve accepts the call, he will receive $1,015.00 (101½) per bond. If he converts, he will receive 18.18 shares of common stock ($1,000 ÷ 55) trading at 60½ per share for a total value of $1,099.89. Steve is better off with almost $1,100 worth of common stock rather than a check for just $1,015. This is an example of a "forced conversion." It is "forced" in the sense that he must convert in order to receive the higher stock value. Not to convert (to merely accept the call) would be to lose money.

CHAPTER 18

BOND AMORTIZATION AND ACCRETION

Speaking very generally, the cost of bonds bought at *premium* prices must be lowered from time to time; this is called *amortization*. Sometimes the cost of bonds bought at *discount* prices must be raised from time to time; this is *accretion*. Thus a bond's "cost," at least for tax purposes, may change over time, because a bondholder's "tax cost basis" may change over time.

The general purpose of such procedures is to properly reflect a fixed-income security's resale or redemption value. This is a rather difficult concept for most investors to grasp—that an investment's "cost" can change at regular intervals after the purchase has been made.

Amortization

Example: A bond with 10 years remaining to maturity is bought at a price of 109.

The bond's purchase price is 109, or $1.090. The premium of $90 over par ($1,090 − $1,000) must be amortized (reduced) each year until maturity. Thus the $90 premium must be scaled down to zero in the tenth year by reducing the cost basis by one-tenth of the premium each year: $90 ÷ 10 years = $9 amortization each year. Thus:

- After one year the bond's tax-cost basis has been reduced to $1,081 ($1,090 − $9).

- At the end of the second year the bond's tax-cost basis is $1,072 [$1,090 − (2 × $ 9)].

- At the end of the third year the cost basis would be $1,063 [$1,090 − (3 × 9)], etc.
- By maturity, the bond's tax cost would be $1,000 [$1,090 − (10 × 9)]. Thus there is no loss when a premium bond is held to maturity as, by that time, the bond's cost basis has been reduced to par.

Accretion

Example: An original-issue discount bond with 20 years to maturity is bought in the primary market at 92 ($920).

Each year until maturity the bond's "cost" for tax purposes will be increased by annualizing the discount. The discount of $80 (the bond's par value of $1,000 less the purchase price of $920) will be spread out over the years to maturity, and the cost basis increased by one-twentieth of the discount ($80 ÷ 20 = $4). Thus:

- At the end of the first year the bond's tax-cost basis will be $924.
- At the end of the second year the basis is $928.
- At the end of each of the remaining years the tax cost basis is increased by $4: $932, $936, and so on.
- By the time of maturity, the cost basis is increased all the way to par.

SELF-TEST

A. What is a bond's tax-cost basis after being bought at 124 (when it had ten years to maturity) and held for 5 years?

B. A 20-year original-issue discount bond is bought in the primary market at 95 and held for 12 years. It is then sold at 97. What is the profit or loss on this transaction?

ANSWERS TO SELF-TEST

A. 112 ($1,120)

The $240 premium must be amortized over the bond's 10-year life. The *annual* amortization is $24. After 5 years the tax-cost basis is $1,120: $1,240 − (5 × $24).

B. $10 loss

The tax-cost basis after 12 years will be the original price increased by 12 times the annual accretion. The annual accretion is arrived at by dividing the discount by the years to maturity. Annual accretion equals $2.50: ($1,000 − $950) ÷ 20 = $2.50 Thus the tax-cost basis after 12 years is $980: $950 + (12 × $2.50). A sale at 97 ($970) will result in a capital loss of $10.

CHAPTER 19

BASIC MARGIN TRANSACTIONS

Trading on margin gives investors "leverage." They can buy a greater number of shares dealing on margin rather than for cash. That's the good news. On the other hand, dealing on margin also increases investor's losses when they choose poorly.

The current initial requirement (minimum down payment) is 50% and has been at this level for quite some time. While the Federal Reserve has the right to change the initial requirement, it hasn't invoked this power for many years and apparently chooses to do other things to affect the economy and trading activity. All our examples in this chapter are based on the current initial requirement of 50%.

Market Value, Debit Balance, Equity

Classically, margin accounts are set up like balance sheets. The net worth (equity) in an account is equal to what it is worth in the marketplace (market value) less whatever the investors owes in way of margin (debit balance):

$$\text{Equity} = \text{Market Value} - \text{Debit Balance}$$

The traditional format for a margin account lists the account's market value (assets), its debit balance (liabilities), and its equity (net worth).

Example: A typical margin account might look like this:

Market Value	$266,000
Debit Balance	− 131,000
Equity	$135,000

This account contains securities with a current market value of $266,000 (market value). The client owes the brokerage firm carrying the account $131,000 (debit balance). The customer's current "stake" in the account is $135,000 (equity).

The margin account is similar to having bought a home, paying part of the purchase price in cash and borrowing the balance from a bank. The account shown reflects the facts that:

- The "house" is now worth $266,000.
- You still owe the bank $131,000 on the mortgage.
- Your interest in the house is now $135,000.

You don't have $135,000 in cash, but you would have it if you sold your home for its current market value and paid off the mortgage. Similarly, the equity in your margin account is the amount you would be entitled to receive if the account were liquidated and all loans outstanding against it were paid off.

Initial Requirement

Let's set up an account from scratch.

Example: An investor opens a margin account and, as her first trade in the account, buys 100 shares of XYZ at 86. Here's what the account will look like after the purchase but before the customer sends any money to the brokerage firm:

Market Value	$8,600	(100 shares at 86)
Debit Balance	− 8,600	(owed to the broker)
Equity	0	

Since the customer has not yet sent in any money, the entire purchase price was laid out by the brokerage firm. At the moment, the customer is in debt to the brokerage firm for the full amount of the purchase. The customer's equity is now zero.

The brokerage firm will send a "margin call" to the customer, asking her to deposit at least $4,300 which is 50% of the purchase price (the *initial requirement*). The customer must send in at least this amount.

Our investor sends in $4,500, which is a little more than the amount of the call. Here's what the account looks like after the customer's check for $4,500 is deposited into the account:

Market Value	$8,600	(100 shares at 86)
Debit Balance	− 4,100	(owed to the broker)
Equity	$4,500	

The customer's $4,500 reduced her debit balance to $4,100 ($8,600 − $4,500). Her equity is now $4,500.

SELF-TEST

A. What is the equity in a margin account with a $38,000 market value and a debit balance of $12,500?

B. The long positions in a margin account are 100 shares of ABC @ 27½ and 200 shares of DEF @ 67¼. The debit balance in the account is $5,150. What is the customer's equity?

ANSWERS TO SELF-TEST

A. $25,500
Market Value ($38,000) − Debit
Balance ($12,500) = Equity ($25,500)

B. $11,050
The account's market value is $16,200
(100 ABC @ 27½ = $2,750 and 200 DEF @ 67¼ = $13,450).

Market Balance	$16,200
Debit Balance	− 5,150
Equity	$11,050

Margin Calls

Margin calls may be issued when a client establishes a position, either long or short. Margin calls are used to request the required minimum deposit (down payment), on a purchase or a short sale, in accordance with the current requirements of the Federal Reserve. A popular misconception is that margin calls are sent out after a market decline. This is not so: *maintenance* calls, not margin calls, are issued when established accounts fall below requirements.

The Federal Reserve is concerned only with the required *initial* deposit. After the appropriate initial deposit is made, the Federal Reserve is effectively out of the picture.

As stated previously, the current initial requirement is 50%. This means that a client must deposit at least 50% of the market value of any securities bought or sold short in a newly opened margin account. An *established* account may have sufficient "buying power" (explained in Chapter 21) to satisfy the requirement in whole or in part. If such be the case, no margin call may have to be sent to the client.

Example: Mrs. Eileen Meehan, as her first transaction in a margin account, orders the purchase of 1,000 shares of RFQ. The shares are bought at 29¼. What is the amount of the margin call that she will be sent?

The market value of 1,000 shares at 29¼ is $29,250. She will be sent a margin call requesting her to deposit 50% of that amount, or $14,625 (0.50 × $29,250). Mrs. Meehan may elect to send in a larger deposit, but her minimum deposit must be at least $14,625.

SELF-TEST

Answer all questions on the assumption that the accounts are newly opened and have no buying power.

A. A client purchases the following in his margin account:

> 100 GHI @ 18½
> 200 JKL @ 36
> 500 MNO @ 88⅛

How much money must he deposit?

B. Ms. Amy Lemel buys 300 PQR @ 59 and sells short 200 STU @ 80 in her margin account. What will be the amount of the margin call generated by this activity?

ANSWERS TO SELF-TEST

A. $26,556.25
The total market value is $53,112.50

100 GHI @ 18½	= $ 1,850
200 JKL @ 36	= 7,200
500 MNO @ 88⅛	= $44,062.50
	$53,112.50

50% of that amount is $26,556.25 (0.50 × $53,112.50 = $26,556.25).

B. $16,850

The total market value of the transactions, both purchases and short sales, are figured in the margin call. Ms. Lemel bought 300 PQR @ 59 ($17,700) and sold short 200 STU @ 80 ($16,000), for a total market value of $33,700 (17,700 + 16,000). She will be sent a margin call for 50% of this total market value, or $16,850 (0.50 × 33,700 = $16,850).

CHAPTER 20

MARGIN: EXCESS EQUITY AND THE SPECIAL MEMORANDUM COUNT (SMA)

After the margin call generated by a purchase or a short sale has been satisfied, the values of the margin account (market value, debit balance, equity) will change constantly. If the securities purchased rise in price, the client's equity increases.

Example: Mr. Rizek opens a margin account and purchases 1,000 shares of VWX at 60. The total value of the purchase is $60,000. Before Mr. Rizek sends any money to the broker, his account will look like this:

Market Value	$60,000	(1,000 VWX @ 60)
Debit Balance	− 60,000	(owed to the broker)
Equity	0	

Mr. Rizek will be sent a margin call for 50% of the market value of the securities he has purchased: 50% of $60,000, or $30,000. After Mr. Rizek has sent in his check for $30,000, the account looks like this:

Market Value	$60,000	(1,000 VWX @ 60)
Debit Balance	− 30,000	(owed to the broker)
Equity	$30,000	

Note: When something "happens" in a margin account—a purchase, a sale, money coming into the account, money going out of the account, the securities in the account going up, the securities in the account going down, any kind of activity at all—two of the margin account's three "values" change. That's a good way to see if you have properly recorded any changes: Make sure that two of the account's three values (market value, debit balance, equity) have changed. Not one value and not three values, just *two*. If you change only one, or all three, then you have made a mistake!

Let's see what happens to a margin account when the security (or securities) in the account rises in price.

Example: If the VWX stock in Mr. Rizek's account goes up to 68 per share, then the account will be:

Market Value	$68,000	(1,000 VWX @ 68)
Debit Balance	− 30,000	(owed to the broker)
Equity	$38,000	

Note: Two values changed. (1) The account's market value went up because of the rise in the price of VWX. (2) The customer's equity increased.

The stock in the account can now be sold for $68,000 and, after the broker takes out the $30,000 debit balance owed him, the customer is entitled to the rest. If the account were to be liquidated, the customer could now be sent a check for $38,000.

Excess Equity

The initial requirement for an account with a $68,000 market value is 50% of that amount, $34,000. That would be the required equity for someone who purchases that much stock. In other words, the *requirement* for a margin account is 50% of the account's current market value.

Example: Bill Grau, a new customer, wants to follow in Mr. Rizek's footsteps and asks his broker to buy him the same securities as in Mr. Rizek's account. Bill is required to deposit 50% of the current value of the account or $34,000. Let's compare the two accounts, side-by-side, after Bill has met his margin call by depositing a check for $34,000 into his account.

	Bill Grau	Steve Rizek
Market Value	$68,000	$68,000
Debit Balance	− 34,000	− 30,000
Equity	$34,000	$38,000

The required equity for an account with a $68,000 long market value is 50% of that amount, or $34,000. We proved that by setting up a new account and figuring how much equity would be required.

Comparing the required equity in Mr. Grau's account with the actual equity in Mr. Rizek's account, we see that Mr. Rizek's account is in excellent shape. He is required to have an equity of $34,000 but in actuality has an equity (thanks to the upward movement in his stock) of $38,000, which is $4,000 greater than the requirement.

This "extra" equity is known officially as *excess equity*, and it is posted to the *special memorandum account* (SMA). Mr. Rizek's excess equity is $4,000 because that is the amount by which the equity in his account ($38,000) exceeds the requirement ($34,000) for an account of that market value. Such comparisons are made by the margin department (now usually called the *credit* department) on a daily basis.

Example: A client buys 100 shares of ABC @ 90 in a newly opened margin account. He deposits the necessary margin after receiving the call. Sometime later ABC increases in price to 120. What is the excess equity in the account after the price increase?

Here's the account just after the initial deposit (while the stock was selling at 90), and then after the price rise to 120.

Stock at 90		
Market Value	$9,000	(100 ABC @ 90)
Debit Balance	− 4,500	(owed the broker)
Equity	$4,500	

Stock at 120		
Market Value	$12,000	(100 ABC @ 120)
Debit Balance	− 4,500	(owed the broker)
	$ 7,500	

The requirement for the account, which now has a market value of $12,000, is 50% of that amount, or $6,000. The account now has an equity of $7,500, which is $1,500 in excess of the requirement. That $1,500 excess over requirement is the excess equity.

SELF-TEST

A. What is the excess equity in an account with a $110,000 market value and a debit balance of $46,000?

B. A margin account has the following long positions:

      100 CDE @ 40

      200 FGH @ 70

      500 IJK @ 20

   1,000 LMN @ 104

and a debit balance of $74,000. What is the account's excess equity?

ANSWERS TO SELF-TEST

A. $9,000

Market Value	$110,000
Debit Balance	− 46,000
Equity	$ 64,000

The account has an equity of $64,000. The requirement is 50% of market value, which is $55,000 (0.50 × $110,000). The actual equity ($64,000), minus the requirement ($55,000), leaves excess equity of $9,000.

B. Zero

There is no excess equity in the account since the actual equity does not exceed the requirement. The account has a market value of $132,000.

100 CDE @ 40	= $ 4,000
200 FGH @ 70 =	14,000
500 IJK @ 20 =	10,000
1,000 LMN @ 104 =	104,000
	$132,000

This market value, less the debit of $74,000, leaves an equity of $58,000. The requirement for an account with a market value of $132,000 is 50% of that amount, or $66,000 (0.50 × $132,000). The equity in the account is less than the requirement so there is no excess equity.

Note: An account with no excess equity is known as a restricted account.

Special Memorandum Account (SMA)

When an account's equity exceeds the requirement, excess equity (SMA) is created. A note is made of such excess equity in a "side" account known as the special memorandum account. Interestingly, once SMA is credited to the account, it remains there until used; it does not disappear even if the account loses the extra market value that created the SMA in the first place! Stocks going up in price in a long margin account create SMA. Once SMA is credited, a later downside movement in stock prices does not decrease the SMA.

That is why some accounts may be restricted (their equity is less than the requirement) but nevertheless have SMA! The SMA was created earlier in the account's history when the stocks that were bought went above their original purchase prices.

SMA is also created, or increased, when:

- A security long in the account is sold. The SMA is automatically credited with one-half the proceeds of any long sale.
- The client sends in cash to reduce the account's debit balance.

Any activity which causes the account's equity to increase above its requirement will increase the SMA.

This SMA is a line of credit. It is a notation to the effect that an account has a credit line, which may be used either to buy additional stock or to make cash withdrawals. While SMA can always be used for additional stock purchases, there are restrictions on using it to withdraw cash. More on this last point later.

Example: An account with an SMA of $12,000 sells $10,000 worth of long stock. What is the new SMA?

Half the proceeds of the sale (0.50 × $10,000 = $5,000) gets added to the previous SMA. Thus $12,000 + $5,000 equals the new SMA of $17,000.

SELF-TEST

A. An account sets up this way:

Market Value	$120,000	
Debit Balance	− 65,000	
Equity	$ 55,000	SMA account—0

The client wishes to reduce his debit balance and sends in a check for $20,000. What is the SMA after the check is credited to the account?

B. A margin account is long 400 CYA @ 64 and 1,000 RFQ @ 55 and has an SMA of $25,000. If the client sells 100 CYA and 200 RFQ, what will be the new SMA?

ANSWERS TO SELF-TEST

A. $15,000

After the client sends in the check for $20,000, the account looks this way:

Market Value	$120,000
Debit Balance	− 45,000
Equity	$ 75,000

Note that the debit balance has been reduced from $65,000 to $45,000 by the cash that was added to the account. The requirement for the account is $60,000 (50% of the market value). The equity in the account now exceeds the requirement by $15,000, which becomes the new SMA.

B. $33,700

The SMA will be increased by 50% of the proceeds of the sales. 100 CYA @ 64 ($6,400) and 200 RFQ @ 55 ($11,000) add up to $17,400 worth of stock sold. One-half of this amount ($8,700) is added to the "old" SMA to give a new SMA of $33,700.

CHAPTER 21

MARGIN: BUYING POWER

A margin account client may buy additional securities—without putting up any more money—in an amount equal to double the SMA. (See Chapter 20 for details on excess equity and SMA.) As long as these additional purchases do not exceed the account's buying power, no margin call will be sent. So the "formula" for figuring buying power is simple: Double the SMA.

$$\text{Buying Power} = 2 \times \text{SMA}$$

Examples: An account with an SMA of $2,500 has a buying power of $5,000. An account with a $13,000 SMA has a buying power of $26,000.

A customer's additional purchases might be less than the buying power available and will reduce the remaining buying power and SMA. Or they may be greater than the available buying power, using it and the SMA entirely and generating a margin call for the amount not covered.

Margin calls are offset, dollar for dollar, by an account's SMA.

Example: An account has an SMA of $3,000 (buying power of $6,000). The investor then buys $1,800 of additional stock. The new purchase would ordinarily generate a margin call for one-half the purchase price, or $900. No margin call will be sent, however, since the SMA will be reduced by the amount of the call; that is, it is reduced by $900 to $2,100. The new SMA is $2,100, and the new buying power is twice that amount, $4,200. The $1,800 purchase reduced the SMA by $900 and the buying power by $1,800.

Full Use of Buying Power

Example: An account has an SMA of $13,500 and a buying power of $27,000. The client wishes to use this buying power to the fullest extent and buys $27,000 worth of additional securities. The new purchase uses up all of his SMA ($13,500) and consequently all of his buying power as well ($27,000). After the new purchases, the account has no SMA and no buying power.

Partial Use of Buying Power

Example: Mr. Paul McQuarrie has an SMA of $12,000 in his account (buying power is therefore $24,000). He then purchases $9,000 worth of additional securities. The new purchases use $4,500 of his SMA and $9,000 of his buying power, reducing SMA to $7,500 and buying power to $15,000.

"Overuse" of Buying Power

Example: An account has an SMA of $12,500 and a buying power of $25,000. An additional $40,000 worth of stock is then purchased. This purchase would normally generate a margin call in the amount of $20,000. The entire SMA, $12,500, can offset only part of the call, and the brokerage firm sends a margin call for the remainder, $7,500. The account then has no SMA and no buying power.

SELF-TEST

A. What is the buying power in an account with an SMA of $3,650?

B. What is the buying power in an account with an SMA of $4,000, which then sells $9,000 worth of stock?

C. An account sets up this way: market value $46,000 with a debit balance of $29,000. Does this account have any buying power?

ANSWERS TO SELF-TEST

A. $7,300
   The buying power is twice the SMA: 2 × $3,650 = $7,300.

B. $17,000

The beginning SMA of $4,000 will be increased by half the proceeds of the stock sold: $4,000 + (0.5 × $9,000) = 4,000 + 4,500 = $8,500. If the new SMA is $8,500, then the new buying power is twice that amount or $17,000.

C. Maybe!

The account is restricted in that the equity of $17,000 (market value of $46,000 − debit balance of $29,000) is less than the 50% requirement of $23,000 (50% of market value). But perhaps the account had been in much better shape previously and still had SMA (and buying power) left over from the "good old days." Remember that an account does not lose SMA when prices decline.

Cash Available

Generally, the SMA can be withdrawn in cash. The exceptions to this rule will be detailed later in this chapter. When the customer withdraws some or all of the SMA in the account, the debit balance increases and the equity decreases. The client can elect:

● Not to use the SMA at all.

● Purchase twice the amount of the SMA without sending in additional funds (buying power).

● Withdraw some or all of it in cash.

After all, since the SMA is a line of credit, it is understandable that clients can borrow more money.

The following account elects to utilize the SMA to the fullest in two ways:

● In the first example by purchasing as much more stock as possible without sending in additional funds.

● In the second example by withdrawing as much additional cash as possible.

Example: Mrs. Lois Sajdak's margin account is as follows:

Market Value	$80,000	SMA	$ 8,000
Debit Balance	− 32,000	Buying Power	$16,000
Equity	$48,000		

Her SMA is $8,000 because her equity exceeds the requirement by that amount [equity $48,000 − requirement $40,000 (50% of market value)].

If Lois decides to utilize her buying power to the fullest by purchasing as much stock as possible, she will purchase $16,000 of additional securities, raising both her market value and her debit balance by that amount. Her account will then show:

Market Value	$96,000	SMA	0
Debit Balance	− 48,000	Buying Power	0
Equity	$48,000		

She will have used up her entire buying power and SMA. Notice that her equity is now 50% of her market value, exactly in line with the requirement.

If instead of purchasing more stock, Lois decides to withdraw as much cash as possible, she will ask that her full SMA ($8,000) be sent to her. This will increase her debit balance and reduce her equity. Her account will now show:

Market Value	$80,000	SMA	0
Debit Balance	− 40,000	Buying Power	0
Equity	$40,000		

Again, she will have used up her entire SMA and buying power. Notice that after this full utilization of SMA, just as after the full utilization of her buying power, the equity in her account is now 50% of her market value, exactly in line with the requirement.

Compare the "original" account with the account as it would appear if it used all the buying power (first example) and as it would appear if it used all the SMA by withdrawing cash. Note that in each case two (not one, not three) of the three values changed. In the first instance we changed the market value and the debit balance; in the second example, the debit balance and the equity.

Exceptions to Cash Withdrawal

There are two important exceptions to the general rule that a margin customer can withdraw the SMA in cash:

● A cash withdrawal may not reduce an account's equity below $2,000.

- A cash withdrawal cannot reduce an account's equity below 25% of market value.

Example: A cash withdrawal may not reduce an account's equity below $2,000. An account appears as follows:

Market Value	$5,000	SMA	$1,000
Debit Balance	− 2,400	Buying Power	$2,000
Equity	$2,600		

If this client wishes to withdraw as much cash as possible, she can only be given $600! To give her more money would cause the account's equity to fall below $2,000. Let's look at the account after the client has been sent the maximum amount of cash, $600.

Market Value	$5,000	SMA	$400
Debit Balance	− $3,000	Buying Power	$800
Equity	$2,000		

Note: The withdrawal of $600 in cash has increased the debit balance and reduced the equity. The SMA is now $ 400 (and the buying power $800), but the customer cannot withdraw any more cash. To do so would cause the equity in the account to fall below $2,000. The account now serves as an example of one in which there is an SMA and buying power, but with no cash available. No cash withdrawals may be made if they reduce equity below 25% of market value.

Example: A cash withdrawal cannot reduce an account's equity below 25% of market value. An account appears as follows:

Market Value	$80,000	SMA	$ 9,000
Debit Balance	− 55,000	Buying Power	$18,000
Equity	$25,000		

If this client wishes to withdraw as much cash as possible, she can only be given $5,000, not the full SMA of $9,000. To give her more than $5,000 would cause the equity in the account to fall below 25% of its market value. Let's look at the account after the client has been sent the maximum amount of cash, $5,000.

Market Value	$80,000	SMA	$4,000
Debit Balance	− 60,000	Buying Power	$8,000
Equity	$20,000		

Note that the withdrawal of $5,000 in cash has increased the debit balance and reduced the equity. The SMA is now $4,000 (and the buying power $8,000), but the customer cannot withdraw any more cash as to do so would cause the equity in the account to fall below 25% of market value. The account's equity is now exactly 25% of its market value. The account still has SMA, but no cash withdrawals may be made.

In summary, the SMA may be withdrawn in cash unless it would cause the equity to fall below $2,000 or below 25% of market value.

SELF-TEST

How much cash may be withdrawn from the following accounts?

A.

Market Value	$56,000	SMA	$10,000
Debit Balance	− 27,000	Buying Power	$20,000
Equity	$29,000		

B.

Market Value	$56,000	SMA	$ 6,000
Debit Balance	− 40,000	Buying Power	$12,000
Equity	$16,000		

C.

Market Value	$5,600	SMA	$1,400
Debit Balance	− 3,500	Buying Power	$2,800
Equity	$2,100		

ANSWERS TO SELF-TEST

A. $10,000

The entire SMA may be withdrawn as doing so would not cause the account to go below $2,000 in equity or the equity to be less than 25% of market value.

Check the answer. Here's the account after the $10,000 withdrawal:

Market Value	$56,000	SMA	0
Debit Balance	− 37,000	Buying Power	0
Equity	$19,000		

The equity did not go below $2,000, and the equity is still above 25% of the market value.

B. $2,000
The customer may only withdraw $2,000 since this will reduce the equity to $14,000, where it will be 25% of market value. Here's the account after the $2,000 withdrawal:

Market Value	$56,000	SMA	$4,000
Debit Balance	− 42,000	Buying Power	$8,000
Equity	$14,000		

The equity in the account is now 25% of the market value, the lowest permissible level.

C. $100
Only $100 may be sent since this will reduce the equity to the lowest permissible minimum of $2,000. Here's the account after the $100 withdrawal:

Market Value	$5,600	SMA	$1,300
Debit Balance	− 3,600	Buying Power	$2,600
Equity	$2,000		

CHAPTER 22

MARGIN: MAINTENANCE REQUIREMENTS FOR LONG ACCOUNTS

The initial margin requirement, as set by the Federal Reserve, is used to determine:

- The minimum deposit that a margin customer must make when creating a position, long or short.
- The margin requirement for an account when determining whether there is any SMA.

This margin requirement, currently 50%, only comes into play when a security is bought or sold short. After the securities are purchased and properly margined, the Fed is no longer concerned.

But other regulatory agencies are. These other institutions include the New York Stock Exchange, the National Association of Securities Dealers, and even the brokerage houses themselves. The rules established by these institutions are designed to ensure that customers do not borrow for the purpose of buying securities and then default on their loans. Defaults can not only endanger the brokerage firm carrying the defaulted account(s), but also, if unchecked, create a domino effect throughout the financial community.

Many individual brokerage firms have their own requirements, which are generally more stringent than those of the NYSE and NASD. These firms' "house rules" can be stiffer than those of the regulatory agencies, but they cannot be more lenient. The reason for such rigorous "house rules" is clear. Since the securities in a brokerage account are the collateral for the debit balance, the lending brokerage firm becomes understandably concerned when the market value of the securities falls below the debit balance. The broker's loan would really be in jeopardy if the securities had to be liquidated and their sale did not bring in enough cash to pay off the debit balance.

Essentially, that's the reason for all the rules on maintenance. They ensure that accounts in danger of becoming undersecured, or unsecured, are handled before they become big problems.

There are different maintenance requirements for long and short accounts. Long maintenance requirements are described in this chapter, short maintenance requirements in Chapter 23.

Long Maintenance Requirements

A long margin account must maintain an equity of at least 25% of the account's market value. That's the long maintenance requirement. The maintenance requirement is the same for this account whatever the debit balance is. It is instead geared to the market value and has nothing to do with any other element of the account, such as debit balance, SMA, or buying power. As long as the equity is 25% or more of the long market value, the account is properly maintained.

Note: The *initial* requirement is 50%, but thereafter the maintenance requirement is 25%.

Example: What is the maintenance requirement for the following account?

Market Value	$120,000	SMA	$10,000
Debit Balance	− 50,000	Buying Power	$20,000
Equity	$70,000		

The maintenance requirement for the account is $30,000. That is, the equity in the account must be at least 25% of the account's long market value. The market value is $120,000 and so the maintenance requirement is 25% of that or $30,000: $0.25 \times \$120,000 = \$30,000$.

Note: Brokerage firms may invoke stricter house requirements, such as 30% or 35%, and most of them do have such a rule.

What happens when an account falls below the 25% maintenance requirement? The customer can bring the account back up to proper levels in three different ways:

1. Depositing cash
2. Depositing additional marginable securities
3. Selling securities in the account

Each of these activities calls for different amounts. The amount of cash deposit necessary to satisfy the call, for instance, is not the same as the value of additional securities to be deposited, and a "sellout" is for a still different amount.

Example: What is the maintenance requirement for the following account:

Market Value	$40,000	SMA	$1,500
Debit Balance	− 33,000	Buying Power	$3,000
	$ 7,000		

The maintenance requirement is $10,000, which is 25% of the account's long market value (0.25 × $40,000 = $10,000). The account has only a $7,000 equity, which is $3,000 less than the $10,000 requirement. This puts the account on maintenance call for $3,000. The account has SMA and buying power, but no cash withdrawals would be permitted.

The maintenance call for $3,000 can be met by:

1. Depositing cash in the same amount as the call: $3,000 in cash.
2. Depositing additional marginable securities worth one-third more than the margin call: 4/3 × the call of $3,000 = $4,000 in additional securities.
3. Selling securities in the account with a market value of four times the amount of the call: $12,000 would have to be sold.

Before the maintenance call is answered, the account looks like this:

Market Value	$40,000
Debit Balance	− 33,000
Equity	$ 7,000

After the maintenance call is met, the account can be affected in three different ways, depending on how the customer responds:

	Deposit of cash ($3,000)	Deposit of marginable securities worth 4/3 the amount of the call (4/3 × $3000 = $4,000)	Sell-out of securities worth 4 × the call (4 × $3,000 = $12,000)
Market Value	$40,000	$44,000	$28,000
Debit Balance	−30,000	−33,000	−21,000
Equity	$10,000	$11,000	$ 7,000

Depositing cash in the amount of the maintenance call reduced the debit balance by $3,000 and increased the equity by $3,000. The equity is now exactly 25% of the market value (0.25 × $40,000 = $10,000) and the account is no longer on maintenance call.

Depositing additional marginable securities into the account, which were worth 4/3 the amount of the maintenance call, raised the market value and equity by $4,000 each. The equity is now exactly 25% of the market value (0.25 × $44,000 = $11,000), and the account is no longer on maintenance call.

Selling $12,000 worth of the securities in the account reduced the market value and the debit balance by $12,000 each. The equity is now exactly 25% of the market value (0.25 × $28,000 = $7,000) and the account is no longer on maintenance call.

SELF-TEST

Use the following account to answer the questions in this Self-Test.

Market Value	$80,000
Debit Balance	− 60,600
Equity	$19,400

A. What is the amount of the maintenance call on this account?

B. How much cash must be deposited to meet the call?

C. If the call were to be met by depositing additional marginable securities, what value of such securities must be deposited?

D. If the call were to be satisfied by selling some securities in the account, what value of such securities must be sold?

ANSWERS TO SELF-TEST

A. $600

The minimum maintenance requirement is 25% of the market value or $20,000: 0.25 × $80,000 = $20,000. The actual equity is just $19,400, which is $600 short of the required amount. That's the amount of the maintenance call.

B. $600

A maintenance call for $600 can be met by depositing that same amount in cash.

C. $800

Meeting a maintenance call by depositing additional marginable securities takes 4/3 (1⅓) of the amount of the call in stock.

$$4/3 × \$600 = \$800$$

That's the amount of "new" stock that would have to be deposited to meet the $600 call.

▶ 4 × 600 ÷ 3 = ◀ **800.** or $800

D. $2,400

Meeting a call by selling out securities in the account requires that positions valued at four times the amount of the call be sold: 4 × $600 = $2,400.

CHAPTER 23

MARGIN: MAINTENANCE REQUIREMENTS FOR SHORT ACCOUNTS

When a client sells stock he or she doesn't own, the transaction is called a *short sale*. To make good the delivery, the brokerage firm borrows shares from someone else. Thus, after the short sale is executed, the client owes the brokerage firm the value of the borrowed stock. Also, since a sale was effected in the account, there is a credit balance for the amount of the short sale.

It's exactly the opposite of a long account. In a long account:

- You *own* the purchased stock and *owe* the debit balance created by the purchase.
- The long stock position is positive $(+)$ and the debit balance is negative $(-)$.

In a short account:

- You *owe* the stock sold short and *own* the credit balance created by the short sale.
- The short stock position is negative $(-)$ and the credit balance is positive $(+)$.

The formula for figuring the equity in a long account is to subtract the debit balance from the market value:

Equity in
Long Margin = Long Market Value − Debit Balance
Account

The formula for figuring the equity in a short margin account is to subtract the short market value from the credit balance.

Equity in
Short Margin = Credit Balance − Short Market Value
Account

Example: The client sells 1,000 shares of PCI, which he doesn't own (a short sale), and the brokerage firm borrows shares from another client's account to make good the delivery. After the order is executed at 80 per share, but before the client sends in any funds, here's what the account looks like:

Credit Balance	$80,000	(the proceeds of the short sale)
Short Market Value	− 80,000	(the borrowed stock owed)
Equity	0	

The account starts out with a credit balance from the short sale. This money came for the sale. The customer did not make delivery of any stock, so the broker borrowed the stock from another source. It is this stock that the customer must ultimately repay.

Initial Requirement

The initial requirement for a short sale is the same as for a long purchase: 50% of the market value.

Example: The $80,000 short sale in the previous example generates a $40,000 margin call (0.50 × $80,000). Just after the short sale but before the client has sent in any funds, the account is as follows:

Credit Balance	$80,000	(the proceeds of the short sale)
Short Market Value	− 80,000	(the borrowed stock owed)
Equity	0	

After the client responds to the margin call by sending in $40,000 in cash the account is as follows:

Credit Balance	$120,000
Short Market Value	− 80,000
Equity	40,000

The credit balance now totals $120,000: $80,000 came for the sale of the stock, and $40,000 cash was sent in to meet the margin call. Now the equity ($40,000) is 50% of the short market value $80,000).

The initial requirement is the same for long and short margin accounts: The beginning equity must equal at least 50% of the market value.

Short Selling Power and SMA

Short accounts that "work" (that is, the short positions go down in price) create SMA and short selling power more quickly than do long accounts. On the other hand, when the stocks rise in price (not a good thing for a short seller), maintenance calls can go out quickly.

Example: Here's what the short account in the previous example looks like if the price of the short position goes down to 70:

Credit Balance	$120,000	
Short Market Value	− 70,000	(current value of borrowed stock)
Equity	$ 50,000	

The margin requirement for an account with a $70,000 market value is 50% of that amount. The account now has a short market value of $70,000, and 50% of that amount is $35,000. Comparing the margin requirement of $35,000 with the actual equity of $50,000 shows that we have an excess equity of $15,000: $50,000 − $35,000. That's the account's SMA—$15,000. Doubling the SMA of $15,000 gives short-selling power of $30,000.

Maintenance Requirements

The maintenance requirements for short positions are much more stringent than for long positions. You will recall that the long maintenance requirement was an equity of 25% of market value. For short positions the requirements depend on the market price of the short positions. Here's the scale of requirements:

Market Price of Short Position	Maintenance Requirement
Up to 2½	$2.50 per share
2½ to 5	100%
5 to 16⅝	$5.00 per share
16¾ and up	30%

Example: What is the maintenance requirement for a margin account with the following short positions?

> 100 ABC @ 2
> 100 DEF @ 4
> 100 GHI @ 6
> 100 JKL @ 20

- The maintenance requirement for ABC (in the "up to 2½" range) is $250 (100 × $2.50).
- The maintenance requirement for DEF (in the 2½ to 5 range) is $400 (100 × $4 × 1).
- The maintenance requirement for GHI (in the 5 to 16⅝ range) is $500 (100 × $5).
- The maintenance requirement for JKL (in the 16¾ and up range) is $600 (100 × 20 × 0.3).

Adding these together gives a total maintenance requirement of $1,750: $250 + $400 + $500 + $600.

Note: The low-priced stocks have very strict requirements. This makes sense. When you short a low-priced stock, there is very little that you can make (after all a stock can only go down to zero). But you can lose a dramatic amount if the stock goes up (theoretically, there is no limit as to how high a stock can go).

SELF-TEST

What is the maintenance requirement for each of the following accounts?

A. Long positions:
> 100 A @ 64½
> 200 B @ 46
> 1,000 C @ 24¾

B. Short positions:
> 100 D @ 50
> 200 E @ 14⅜
> 100 F @ 3⅞
> 1,000 G @ 1½

ANSWERS TO SELF-TEST

A. $10,100

The maintenance requirement is 25% of the total long market value.

100 A @ 64½	= $ 6,450
200 B @ 46	= 9,200
1,000 C @ 24¾	= $24,750
	$40,400
0.25 × $40,400	= $10,100

▶ 100 × 64.5 M+ 200 × 46 M+ 1000 × 24.75 M+
            Mrc × 25 ÷ 100 = ◀ **10100.** or $10,100.

B. $5,387.50

The maintenance requirement is different for each of the short positions listed:

        100 D @ 50   − 30% or $1,500
        200 E @ 14⅜ − $5.00 per share or $1,000
        100 F @ 3⅞ − 100% or $387.50
    1,000 G @ 1½ − $2.50 per share or $2,500

These individual maintenance requirements total $5,387.50.

CHAPTER 24

MARGIN: MAINTENANCE EXCESS

An account's *maintenance excess*, if any, is the amount by which the actual equity exceeds the maintenance requirement. As you have seen, when the account is below the maintenance requirement, the brokerage firm sends a maintenance call.

The calculation for maintenance excess is quite simple: You simply compare the equity to the maintenance requirement.

Examples: A long margin account sets up as follows:

Long Market Value	$50,000
Debit Balance	− 18,000
Equity	$32,000

- The maintenance requirement is 25% of the long market value, or $12,500: 0.25 × $50,000.

- The actual equity is $32,000, which is $19,500 greater than the requirement: $32,000 − $12,500.

The maintenance excess is $19,500.

Example: A short margin account sets up this way:

Credit Balance	$44,000	
Short Market Value	− 25,000	(1,000 shares @ 25)
Equity	$19,000	

- The maintenance requirement is 30% of the short market value, or $7,500: 0.30 × $25,000.
- The actual equity is $19,000, which is $11,500 greater than the requirement: $19,000 − $7,500.

The maintenance excess is $11,500.

SELF-TEST

A. What is the maintenance excess for a long margin account with a market value of $80,000 and a debit balance of $50,000?

B. What is the maintenance excess for a short margin account with a market value of $40,000 and a credit balance of $55,000? (All short positions have a market value of 16¾ or higher.)

C. What is the maintenance excess for a long margin account with a market value of $24,000 and a debit balance of $20,000?

ANSWERS TO SELF-TEST

A. $10,000

The maintenance requirement is $20,000: 25% of the $80,000 market value. The actual equity is $30,000: $80,000 market value − $50,000 debit balance. The equity exceeds the requirement by $10,000.

B. $3,000

The maintenance requirement is $12,000: 30% of the $40,000 short market value. The actual equity is $15,000: $55,000 credit balance − $40,000 short market value. The equity exceeds the requirement by $3,000.

C. Zero

There is no maintenance excess. The maintenance requirement is 25% of the long market value, or $6,000: 0.25 × $24,000. The actual equity is only $4,000: market value of $24,000 − debit of $20,000. Thus the equity is less than the requirement and the account is in fact on maintenance call for $2,000.

CHAPTER 25

PRICING OPTIONS

Equity Options

Equity options are priced, like stocks, in "points" and "eighths" (1/8s). Lower-priced options may trade in sixteenths (1/16s). The following table lists the decimal equivalents for sixteenths:

1/16 = 0.0625	9/16 = 0.5625
3/16 = 0.1875	11/16 = 0.6875
5/16 = 0.3125	13/16 = 0.8125
7/16 = 0.4375	15/16 = 0.9375

The "even" sixteenths trade as eighths:

1/8 (2/16) = 0.125	5/8 (10/16) = 0.625
1/4 (4/16) = 0.25	3/4 (12/16) = 0.75
3/8 (6/16) = 0.375	7/8 (14/16) = 0.875
1/2 (8/16) = 0.50	

It is not necessary to memorize the decimal equivalents for sixteenths. You can find them by using the calculator:

CALCULATOR GUIDE

1/16 = ▶ 1 ÷ 16 = ◀ **0.0625** or 0.0625

3/16 = ▶ 3 ÷ 16 = ◀ **0.1875** or 0.1875 etc.

Each equity option covers 100 shares of the underlying stock. The price quoted in the newspaper must be multiplied by 100 to arrive at the *price*, or actual dollar cost of the equity option.

Examples:

- A put or call selling for "1½" costs $150 (1.5 × 100).

- An option priced at "4¾" sells for $475 (4.75 × 100).

- An option trading at "1³⁄₁₆" sells for $118.75 (1.1875 × 100).

A call option's *aggregate exercise price* is the amount of cash that must be put up if and when the option is exercised. This is the actual cost for exercising the option. Again, as we did when figuring the cost of the option itself, we must multiply the strike price by 100 to arrive at the aggregate exercise price.

Example: The aggregate exercise price for a call with a strike price of 35 would be $3,500: 35 × 100.

Use Figure 25-1 for both the examples and the self-test.

Figure 25-1
Listed Options Quotations

(Courtesy of *The Wall Street Journal*, September 27, 1991.)

Examples: The cost of 2 Fluor Oct 45 puts is $625. Each put for 100 shares is quoted at 3⅛. A single put sells for $312.50 (100 × 3.125), and 2 puts cost twice that, or $625.

Four Dow Ch Nov 50 calls sell for $1,400. Each call covering 100 shares is quoted at 3½. So a single call sells for $350 (100 × 3.5), and four puts would cost four times that amount, or $1,400.

The aggregate exercise price for exercising these four calls is $20,000. With the strike price at 50, the aggregate exercise price for each call is $5,000 (100 × $50) and $20,000 for all four calls.

SELF-TEST

A. What would be the cost of 10 Fed Exp Jan 30 calls?

B. How much would 5 Bruns Dec 12½ puts cost?

ANSWERS TO SELF-TEST

A. $6,500

The calls are listed at 6½, which means $650 for 1 call and $6,500 for 10 calls.

B. $468.75

The puts are listed at 15/16, which works out to $93.75 for 1 put and $468.75 for 5 puts.

Debt Options

The only active debt options currently (early 1992) traded are shown in Figure 25-2.

Note: These options trade in eighths and sixteenths as do equity options.

Example: Use Figure 25-2.

● The Dec 47½ short-term interest rate calls are listed at 2⅛. A single call sells for $212.50 and 10 calls for $2,125.00.

● The Jan 75 long-term interest rate puts are listed at 11/16. A single put costs $68.75 and 10 puts cost $687.50.

Up to the late eighties, the CBOE traded options on U.S. Treasury bonds and notes. (It is possible that these options

Figure 25-2
Interest Rate Instruments

OPTIONS

Thursday, October 24, 1991
For Notes and Bonds, decimals in closing prices represent 32nds; 1.01 means 1 1/32. For Bills, decimals in closing prices represent basis points; $25 per .01.

Chicago Board Options Exchange

OPTIONS ON SHORT-TERM INTEREST RATES

Strike	Calls—Last			Puts—Last		
Price	Nov	Dec	Jan	Nov	Dec	Jan
47½	....	2⅛	...	....	....	....
50	....	¾	13/16	....	.. .	....
52½	....	....	3/16	....	....	....

Total call volume 60   Total call open int. 1,499
Total put volume 0   Total put open int. 96
IRX levels: High 50.40; Low 49.70; Close 49.70, −0.70

OPTIONS ON LONG-TERM INTEREST RATES

Strike	Calls—Last			Puts—Last		
Price	Nov	Dec	Jan	Nov	Dec	Jan
75	....	2⅞	.. .	....	9/16	11/16

Total call volume 300   Total call open int. 1,232
Total put volume 144   Total put open int. 875
LTX levels: High 77.00; Low 76.62; Close 76.73, −0.56

(Courtesy of *The Wall Street Journal*, October 25, 1991.)

may once again be traded in the future and may therefore appear on the series 7 exam.) Refer to Figure 25-3.

As you can see from the figure, these options were not very actively traded. Their pricing is unique in that they are expressed in points and 32nds. The contract size is $100,000 (100M), and the strike prices and premiums are expressed in points and thirty-seconds as a percent of the contract size.

Figure 25-3
CBOE Quotations

Chicago Board Options Exchange
U.S. Treasury Bond—$100,000 Principal Value

Underlying Issue	Strike Price	Calls—Last			Puts—Last		
		April	May	June	April	May	June
8⅞% due 2/2019	97½	0.21					
9% due 11/2018	98				0.09		
	99				1.04		
	99½	0.16					

3 p.m. prices of underlying issues supplied by The Chicago Corp.: T-Bonds 8⅞% 97.09; 9% 98.13

- For T-notes and T-bonds, decimals in closing prices represent 32nds. For example, 1.01 means 1 1/32.

- For T-bills, decimals in closing prices represent basis points—$25 per 0.01, as an example.

Examples: The 97½ strike price represents $97,500 (0.975 × $100,000), and the 99 strike price represents $99,000 (0.99 × $100,000).

The few option prices (premiums) shown are also in points and thirty-seconds, and their dollar costs are expressed as a percent of the contract size.

Examples: The 8⅞% bonds due in 2019 show an April 97½ call price of ''0.21.''

- 0.21 is equal to 21/32nds or 0.65625.
- Expressed as a percent, 0.65625 becomes 0.0065625 (moving the decimal point two places to the left converts to a percent).
- The dollar cost of the option is $656.25 (0.0065625 × $100,000).

The price for one 97½ April call option trading at 0.21 is $656.25.

The April puts on the 9% bonds with a 98 strike price are quoted at ''0.09.''

- 0.09 equals 9/32nds or 0.28125.
- Expressed as a percent, 0.28125 is 0.0028125.
- Multiplied by $100,000, 0.0028125 gives a dollar price of $281.25.

SELF-TEST

A. What is the dollar cost for 5 April 99 puts on the 9% bond?

B. What is the dollar cost for 10 April 99½ calls on the 9% bond?

ANSWERS TO SELF-TEST

A. $5,625   (1.04 = 1⁴/₃₂ or 1.125)
Expressed as a percent, 1.125 = 0.01125 (move the decimal point two places to the left). Multiplying by $100,000 gives $1,125 for 1 option and $5,625 for 5 options.

▶ 1.125 ÷ 100 × 100000 × 5 = ◀ **5625.** or $5,625.

B. $5,000   (0.16 = 16/32 = 1/2 or 0.5)

Expressed as a percent, 0.5 = 0.005. Multiplying by $100,000 gives $500 for 1 option and $5,000 for 10 options.

▶ 0.5 ÷ 100 × 100000 × 10 = ◀ **5000.** or $5,000.

Foreign Currency Options

The value of the underlying currency, the premiums (options prices), and the strike prices for the currently traded foreign currency options are all expressed in cents or hundredths of cents. Australian Dollars, British Pounds, German Marks, and Swiss Francs are traded in cents per unit, while Japanese Yen are traded in hundredths of cents per unit. (At one time, French Francs—no longer active—were traded in tenths of cents per unit.) To convert strike prices to dollars and cents (except for Japanese Yen), divide the strike price by 100. It may be easier for you simply to move the decimal point two places to the left. Refer to Figure 25-4.

Figure 25-4
Currency Options Quotations

FUTURES

	Open	High	Low	Settle	Change	Lifetime High	Lifetime Low	Open Interest
JAPAN YEN (IMM)—12.5 million yen; $ per yen (.00)								
Dec	.7678	.7706	.7673	.7705	− .0002	.7770	.6997	76,281
Mr92	.7676	.7696	.7697	.7697	− .0001	.7718	.7000	1,519
June	....	....	.7699	.7699	....	.7705	.7015	383
Sept	....	....	.7708	+ .0001	.7710	.7265	732
Dec	....	....	.7720	+ .0002	.7700	.7512	1,147

Est vol 23,237; vol Thur 19,739; open int 80,062, +1,129.

	Open	High	Low	Settle	Change	Lifetime High	Lifetime Low	Open Interest
DEUTSCHEMARK (IMM)—125,000 marks; $ per mark								
Dec	.5861	.5897	.5861	.5896	+ .0056	.6770	.5365	59,461
Mr92	.5815	.5842	.5811	.5841	+ .0056	.5923	.5353	2,916
June	....	....	.5789	+ .0056	.5868	.5322	234

Est vol 38,836; vol Thur 34,221; open int 62,613, +1,846.

	Open	High	Low	Settle	Change	Lifetime High	Lifetime Low	Open Interest
CANADIAN DOLLAR (IMM)—100,000 dlrs.; $ per Can $								
Dec	.8822	.8834	.8817	.8831	+ .0014	.8834	.8175	26,108
Mr92	.8772	.8782	.8768	.8780	+ .0014	.8782	.8253	2,740
June	.8723	.8735	.8722	.8734	+ .0014	.8735	.8330	463

Est vol 4,336; vol Thur 4,710; open int 29,435, +599.

	Open	High	Low	Settle	Change	Lifetime High	Lifetime Low	Open Interest
BRITISH POUND (IMM)—62,500 pds.; $ per pound								
Dec	1.7040	1.7150	1.7040	1.7144	+.0158	1.7900	1.5670	20,451
Mr92	1.6850	1.6970	1.6850	1.6960	+.0156	1.7200	1.5560	1,347

Est vol 16,471; vol Thur 9,964; open int 21,807, +309.

	Open	High	Low	Settle	Change	Lifetime High	Lifetime Low	Open Interest
SWISS FRANC (IMM)—125,000 francs; $ per franc								
Dec	.6724	.6755	.6716	.6754	+ .0058	.8090	.6205	25,510
Mr92	.6672	.6710	.6672	.6708	+ .0058	.6900	.6225	580

Est vol 17,159; vol Thur 15,025; open int 26,138, +1,457.

	Open	High	Low	Settle	Change	Lifetime High	Lifetime Low	Open Interest
AUSTRALIAN DOLLAR (IMM)—100,000 dlrs.; $ per A.$								
Dec	.7932	.7949	.7930	.7949	+ .0004	.7960	.7380	1,739

Est vol 56; vol Thur 217; open int 1,743, +82.

	Open	High	Low	Settle	Change	Lifetime High	Lifetime Low	Open Interest
U.S. DOLLAR INDEX (FINEX)—500 times USDX								
Dec	91.59	91.62	91.06	91.11	− .65	98.96	90.38	5,880
Mr92	92.61	92.52	92.12	92.16	− .63	98.90	91.49	642

Est vol 3,749; vol Thur 2,529; open int 6,542, −943.
The index: High 90.81; Low 90.35; Close 90.35 −.62

(Courtesy of *The Wall Street Journal*, October 21, 1991.)

Examples: The strike prices for British Pounds range from 152½ to 180, that is, 152½ to 180 *cents.* Either figure, multiplied by 100, translates to a price of $1.525 to $1.80. (You can also just move the decimal place left two places.)

The Canadian Dollar strike prices are 85½, 87, 87½, 88, and 89½. These are equal to $0.855, $0.87, $0.875, $0.88 and $0.895.

CALCULATOR GUIDE

▶ 85.5 ÷ 100 = ◀ **0.855** or $0.855

▶ 87 ÷ 100 = ◀ **0.87** or $0.87

▶ 87.5 ÷ 100 = ◀ **0.875** or $0.875

▶ 88 ÷ 100 = ◀ **0.88** or $0.88

▶ 89.5 ÷ 100 = ◀ **0.895** or $0.895

In contrast with equity options, which have a unit of trading of 100, trading units for currency options vary from 31,250 (British Pounds) to 6,250,000 (Japanese Yen). It is not necessary to memorize these trading units; they are shown in the daily price listings (see Figure 25-4).

The market prices for the various currencies—the *underlying*—are equivalent to the "closing prices" of the underlying stocks for equity options. Again, these prices are in cents per unit for British Pounds, Canadian Dollars, German Marks, and Swiss Francs; in hundredths of cents per unit for Japanese Yen.

Examples: Refer to Figure 25-4.

● German Marks had an underlying price of 58.71; that is, 58.71 cents per Mark, or $0.5871.

● The British Pounds were priced at 170.97 or $1.7097 per Pound.

● Japanese Yen are priced at 77.10, which represents hundredths of cents per unit. This translates to 0.771 cents, or $0.00771, per Yen (slightly less than eight tenths of a cent per Yen).

To calculate the cost of purchasing a currency option, multiply the unit of trading by the premium. Remember that the premiums are in cents or hundredths of cents per unit.

Example: In Figure 25-4, the March puts on the British Pound with a striking price of 167½ are quoted at 4.07. To establish the cost of one such put, multiply the unit of trading (31,250) by the premium ($0.0407): 31,250 × $0.0407 = $1,271.88.

CALCULATOR GUIDE

▶ 31250 × 4.07 ÷ 100 = ◀ **1271.875** or $1,271.88

SELF-TEST

Use Figure 25-4 to answer the following questions.

A. What is the dollar cost for 5 Swiss Francs 78½ March calls?

B. How much do 10 Japanese Yen 80 November calls cost?

ANSWERS TO SELF-TEST

A. $4,437.50

The unit of trading is 62,500 francs. The price for the 78½ March calls is 1.42, or $0.0142. Multiplying the two figures gives the cost for a single call. Then multiplying by 5 gives the cost for 5 calls: 62,500 × $0.0142 × 5 = $4437.50.

Note that the quote of 1.42 can be converted to dollars and cents by moving the decimal two places to the left.

▶ 62500 × 1.42 ÷ 100 × 5 = ◀ **4437.5** or $4,437.50

B. $1,250

The unit of trading is 6,250,000 and the price for the November calls is 0.20. That price means 2/10 of 1/100 of a cent per unit. The price per unit is $0.00002. Multiplying the unit of trading by the price gives the cost of a single call; then multiply by 10 to arrive at the cost for all 10 calls.

6,250,000 × $0.00002 × 10 = $1,250

▶ 6250000 × 0.20 ÷ 10000 × 10 = ◀ **1250.** or $1,250.

Note: To convert Yen quotes to dollars and cents, it's a lot simpler to move the decimal *four* places to the left.

Index Options

As of early 1992, the most actively traded index option was the S&P 100 Index. The trading volume in this option alone exceeded the volume for all the other index options combined.

Index options, like equity options, are traded in points and 8ths (16ths for lower-priced options). The most common multiplier for index options is 100, just as it is for equity options. Therefore, to arrive at the dollar price of an index option, multiply the quoted price (premium) by 100. Refer to Figure 25-5.

Examples:

- The S&P 100 370 October puts are quoted at 4¼. The cost of one such put is $425: 4.25 × 100.
- The S&P 100 345 November calls are quoted at 22⅝. The cost of one call is $2,262.50: 22.625 × 100.

SELF-TEST

A. What is the dollar cost of 1 S&P 100 Index December call option with a 385 strike price?

B. What is the dollar cost for 10 S&P 100 Index October puts with a 360 strike price?

ANSWERS TO SELF-TEST

A. $262.50
The premium of 2⅝ is multiplied by 100.

▶ 2.625 × 100 = ◀ **262.5** or $262.50

B. $437.50 (7/16 × 100 × 10 = $437.50)

▶ 7 ÷ 16 × 100 × 10 = ◀ **437.5** or $437.50

Figure 25-5
Index Options Quotations

Chicago Board

S&P 100 INDEX-$100 times index

Strike Price	Calls—Last Oct	Calls—Last Nov	Calls—Last Dec	Puts—Last Oct	Puts—Last Nov	Puts—Last Dec
335	31¾	....	....	1/16	⅝	....
340	26½	27¼	28½	1/16	13/16	2½
345	21¾	22⅝	26	1/16	1 3/16	3⅜
350	16⅞	18½	20¼	⅛	1 11/16	4⅛
355	11⅞	14⅛	18¼	3/16	2½	5⅜
360	7	10⅜	14¾	7/16	3⅞	6⅞
365	2 15/16	7⅛	11⅛	1⅜	5¾	8¾
370	13/16	4½	8¼	4¼	8⅛	11⅜
375	3/16	2½	6	9	11¼	14¼
380	1/16	1⅜	4⅜	13⅝	16	16¾
385	1/16	¾	2⅝	18¼	....	....
390	....	⅜	1¾	26½	....	25
395	....	¼	....	....	....	....

Total call volume 203,454 Total call open int. 406,020
Total put volume 149,700 Total put open int. 401,559
The index: High 367.65; Low 362.71; Close 366.81, +3.30

(Courtesy of *The Wall Street Journal*, October 16, 1991.)

CHAPTER 26

OPTIONS MARGIN

Margin requirements are reduced for out-of-the-money options. Let's review the concept of in-, at-, or out-of-the-money. In general, options are in-the-money when it is profitable to exercise them and out-of-the-money when it is not profitable to exercise them. In-the-money options have *intrinsic value*, while at-the-money and out-of-the-money options have no intrinsic value.

Calls

A call option is:

- *In-the-money* when it is profitable to exercise the option and to immediately resell the underlying in the secondary market. This condition prevails when the call's strike price is less than the current market price for the underlying.

- *Out-of-the-money* when its strike price is higher than the underlying's market price. Someone exercising the call and immediately reselling in the secondary market suffers a loss.

- *At-the-money* when the underlying is selling at the strike price. Someone who exercises the call and immediately resells in the secondary market has neither a profit nor a loss.

Examples:

- An XYZ 50 call is in-the-money when XYZ is selling in the open market for any price higher than 50. If XYZ is trading at 53½, then the 50 call option is in-the-money by 3½ points. The in-the-money value is known as *intrinsic value*. Note that the price (premium) of the option is immaterial.

- An XYZ 50 call is out-of-the-money when XYZ is trading at less than 50. If XYZ is 46¼, then the 50 call is 3¾ points out-of-the-money. The option has no intrinsic value. Again, the price of the option itself makes no difference.

- If XYZ is trading exactly at 50, then the 50 call is at-the-money. Someone exercising the call and immediately selling the stock shows neither a profit nor a loss. The call (like the out-of-the-money call) has no intrinsic value.

Puts

A put is:

- *In-the-money* when the strike price is higher than the underlying's market price.

- *Out-of-the-money* when the strike price is lower than the underlying's market price.

- *At-the-money* when the strike price and the market price are equal.

Examples: An ABC 35 put is:

- 2½ points in-the-money when ABC is trading at 32½.
- 3¼ points out-of-the-money when ABC is 38¼.
- At-the-money when ABC is trading at 35.

Margining Equity Options

Long options cannot be margined; they have no loan value and must be paid for in full. Only short options may be margined.

The margin requirement for short equity options is 20% of the value of the underlying stock (reduced by any out-of-the-money amount, but not less than 10% of the underlying's value) plus the premium.

Note: You must calculate 20% of the market value of the underlying stock, not 20% of the value of the strike price.

Examples: What is the margin requirement for 1 short 50 call when the underlying stock is trading at 51½ and the option is trading at 3/4?

- 20% of the stock's market price is $1,030: 0.2 × $5,150.
- Since the option is in-the-money, the basic requirement cannot be reduced. Adding the premium gives a total requirement of $1,105 ($1,030 + $75).

What is the margin requirement for a short 95 put when the premium is 4¼ and the underlying is trading at 97?

- 20% of the underlying is $1,940: 0.2 × $9,700.
- The option is out-of-the-money by 2 points, so the basic requirement of $1,940 may be reduced by $200 to $1,740. Adding the premium of 4¼ gives a total margin requirement of $2,165 ($1,740 + $425).

What is the margin requirement for a short 20 call when the underlying is trading at 15½ and the option is priced at 1/4?

- 20% of the underlying is $310: 0.2 × $1,550.
- The option is out-of-the-money by 4½ points, so the basic requirement can be reduced, but not to less than 10% of the underlying's value. 10% of market value is $155, so we can reduce the basic requirement only to that level. Adding the premium gives a total margin requirement of $180 ($155 + $25).

SELF-TEST

A. What is the margin requirement for five CYA 15 short calls when CYA is trading at 16 and the calls are at 2½?

B. What is the margin requirement for 10 RFQ 30 short puts when RFQ is trading at 31½ and the puts are at 3/8?

ANSWERS TO SELF-TEST

A. $2,850

For a single option, the requirement is 20% of the underlying stock's current market value, or $320 (0.2 × $1,600). Since the options are in-the-money, the basic requirement cannot be reduced. Adding the premium gives a total requirement of $570 for a single option and $2,850 for 5 options.

▶ 20 ÷ 100 × 16 × 100   M+   2.5 × 100   M+   Mrc × 5
                                = ◀ **2850.** or $2,850.

B. $5,175

For a single option, the requirement is 20% of the underlying stock's current market value, or $630 (0.2 ×
$3,150). Since the options are 1½ points out-of-the-
money, the basic requirement can be reduced by $150 to
$480. Adding the premium of $37.50 gives a total requirement of $517.50 for a single option and $5,175 for
10 options.

▶ 20 ÷ 100× 31.5 × 100   M+ 1.5 × 100   M− 0.375 × 100
                   M+ Mrc × 10 = ◀ **5175.** or $5,175.

Margining Debt Options

For uncovered short debt options, the margin requirement is
the premium plus $3,000 for Treasury notes and $3,500 for
Treasury bonds. The requirement on the bonds is understandably higher because of their longer length to maturity.

The margin requirement is reduced for out-of-the-money
options, but in no event may the requirement be less than the
premium plus $500.

Example: What is the margin requirement for an uncovered
short call option on Treasury bonds with a 97½ strike price
when the closing price is 97.24 and the option is trading at
0.29?

● The premium is 29 ÷ 32nds, or 0.90625.

● Expressed as a percent, 0.90625 becomes 0.0090625.

● Multiplying by the $100,000 contract size gives a dollar
  value for this premium of $906.25.

● The option is in-the-money: The strike price is 97½ and
  the underlying is 97.24, which equals 97¾. Therefore, the
  basic requirement cannot be reduced. Adding $3,500
  gives a margin requirement of $4,406.25 ($3,500 +
  $906.25).

Margining Foreign Currency Options

For short foreign currency options, the required margin is the
premium plus 4.0% of the value of the underlying. Margin
may be reduced for out-of-the-money options, but never
below the premium plus 0.75% of the underlying.

Example: Refer to Figure 26-1. What is the required margin for an uncovered short position in 10 German Marks December 60 puts?

The puts are in-the-money, since the strike price is 60 and the underlying is 58.71. Therefore, the basic requirement cannot be reduced. The margin is figured by adding 4% of the underlying's market value to the premium:

- To calculate the value of the underlying, multiply the market price by the unit of trading: $0.5871 × 62,500 = $36,693.75.

- 4% of this value is $1,467.75 (0.04 × $36,693.75).

- Multiply the premium of 1.73 ($0.0173) by the German Marks trading unit of 62,500: 0.0173 × 62,500 = $1,081.25.

- 4% of the underlying value ($1,467.75), added to the premium ($1,081.25), gives the total requirement for a single option: $2,549.

- The requirement for 10 such options would be $25,490 (10 × $2,549).

Figure 26-1
Currency Options Quotations

Option & Underlying	Strike Price	Calls–Last			Puts–Last		
		Nov	Dec	Mar	Nov	Dec	Mar
50,000 Australian Dollars-cents per unit.							
ADollr.....	78	r	r	r	0.21	r	r
79.72	79	1.07	r	r	0.47	r	r
31,250 British Pounds-cents per unit.							
BPound ..	152½	r	r	r	r	r	0.60
170.97 ..	165	r	r	r	0.45	1.09	3.50
170.97 ..	167½	r	r	r	r	r	4.07
170.97 ..	170	2.95	r	r	1.40	r	5.20
170.97 ..	172½	1.75	r	3.70	2.92	r	6.65
170.97 ..	175	0.83	r	r	4.09	r	8.15
170.97 ..	177½	0.40	r	r	r	r	r
170.97 ..	180	0.20	r	r	r	r	r
50,000 Canadian Dollars-cents per unit.							
CDollr.....	85½	r	r	r	r	0.02	r
88.61 ...	87	r	r	r	r	0.11	r
88.61	87½	r	r	r	0.09	r	r
88.61	88	r	r	r	0.17	0.25	r
88.61	89½	0.04	r	r	r	r	r
62,500 German Marks-European Style							
DMark	58	r	r	r	0.39	r	r
58.71	60	0.36	r	r	r	r	r
62,500 German Marks-cents per unit.							
DMark	53	r	r	r	r	0.03	r
58.71	55	r	r	r	r	0.11	r
58.71	55½	r	r	r	s	0.15	s
58.71	56	r	r	r	r	0.22	r
58.71	56½	r	r	r	s	0.13	0.31
58.71	57	r	r	r	0.17	0.55	1.29
58.71	57½	r	r	r	s	0.25	0.55	r
58.71	58	1.32	r	r	s	0.34	0.76	r
58.71	58½	r	r	r	s	0.50	0.96	s
58.71	59	0.79	1.06	r	r	0.69	1.13	r
58.71	60	0.40	r	r	r	1.34	1.73	r
58.71	60½	r	0.45	s	r	r	r	s

(Courtesy of *The Wall Street Journal,* October 21, 1991.)

Margining Index Options

Margin required for short index options is the premium plus:

- Either 20% of the index value (narrow-based index).
- Or 15% of the index value (broad-based index).

As is the case with all other types of options, the basic requirement can be reduced for out-of-the-money options, but it can be no lower than the premium plus 10% of the index value.

Example: What is the required margin for a short S&P 100 Index 360 call when the premium is 2⅞ and the index price is 361.08?

- The index price is 361.08, which translates to $36,108.
- Since we are dealing with a broad-based index, we use 15% of this value as the basic requirement: $0.15 \times \$36,108 = \$5,416.20$.
- The premium, in dollars, is $287.50.
- Adding the premium to 15% of the index value gives a total margin requirement of $5,703.70.

Note: Series 7 test-takers, this chapter has dealt with the figuration of the margin requirement for various short option positions. If you are asked for the margin call rather than for the margin requirement, you do not add in the premium. Keep in mind that when you sell an option, your account is credited with the proceeds of that sale. This puts money into the account, which satisfies at least part of the requirement. The customer thus has to send in, in cash, only the amount by which the total margin requirement exceeds the premium. The requirement includes the premium; the call (the amount of cash the customer must deposit) excludes the premium.

CHAPTER 27

FINANCIAL RATIOS

The series 7 examination does not place much emphasis on financial ratios. Included in this chapter are only the more important ones that might be tested.

Use the balance sheet in Figure 27-1 and the income statement in Figure 27-2 for all the formulas and examples presented. For the Self-Test, you will use a different set of statements.

Working Capital

Working capital, a dollar figure, measures the excess of current assets over current liabilities.

Working Capital = Current Assets − Current Liabilities

Broadly speaking, *current assets* include cash and items that will become cash within the coming year. *Current liabilities* include the amounts that the company expects to pay out within the year. There should be an excess of incoming cash over expected expenses.

Example: See Figure 27-1.

Working Capital = Current Assets − Current Liabilities
= $4,545,000 − $2,405,000
= $2,140,000

Marobeth's working capital is $2,140,000.

Figure 27-1

Marobeth Corporation
Balance Sheet
December 31, 1992

CURRENT ASSETS			**CURRENT LIABILITIES**	
Cash	$ 450,000		Cash div. payable	$ 150,000
Marketable Secs.	95,000		Accounts payable	955,000
Accounts Rec.	1,885,000		Accrued expenses	1,035,000
Inventory	2,115,000		Accrued taxes	265,000
	$ 4,545,000			$2,405,000
FIXED ASSETS			**LONG-TERM LIABILITIES**	
Property & plant	3,350,000		9% bonds due 2006	1,000,000
Equipment	1,195,000		TOTAL LIABILITIES	3,405,000
Prepaid expenses	755,000		**NET WORTH**	
	5,300,000		7% Pfd. ($100 par)	500,000
			Common stk. ($1 par)	1,900,000
INTANGIBLE ASSETS			Capital surplus	300,000
Goodwill	950,000		Retained earnings	4,690,000
			TOTAL NET WORTH	7,390,000
			TOTAL LIABILITIES	
TOTAL ASSETS	$10,795,000		AND NET WORTH	10,795,000

Current Ratio

The *current ratio* shows the relationship between current assets and current liabilities—how many times the current assets are greater than the current liabilities. It is expressed as a ratio, not in dollars and cents.

Current Ratio = Current Assets ÷ Current Liabilities

Example: See Figure 27-1.

$$
\begin{aligned}
\text{Current Ratio} &= \text{Current Assets} \div \text{Current Liabilities} \\
&= \$4,545,000 \div \$2,405,000 \\
&= 1.9 \text{ to } 1
\end{aligned}
$$

Marobeth's current ratio is 1.9 to 1 (or 1.9:1).

CALCULATOR GUIDE

▶ 4545000 ÷ 2405000 = ◀ **1.8898128** or 1.9 to 1

Quick Assets

Expressed as a dollar figure, *quick assets* indicates the total amount of money that a company could muster on short notice. Typically it includes all current assets except inventory. Inventory is excluded, because other current asset items are rather easily converted to cash, while inventories are considered relatively illiquid.

Quick Assets = Current Assets − Inventory

Example: See Figure 27-1.

$$
\begin{aligned}
\text{Quick Assets} &= \text{Current Assets} - \text{Inventory} \\
&= \$4,545,000 - \$ \$2,115,000 \\
&= \$2,430,000
\end{aligned}
$$

Marobeth's quick assets are $2,430,000.

Quick Asset Ratio

Sometimes called the liquidity ratio or acid test ratio, the *quick asset ratio* measures a company's ability to remain solvent—to quickly pay its near-term obligations.

Quick Asset Ratio = Quick Assets ÷ Current Liabilities

Example: See Figure 27-1.

Quick Asset Ratio = Quick Assets ÷ Current Liabilities
= \$2,430,000 ÷ \$2,405,000
= 1.0 to 1

The quick asset ratio for Marobeth is 1.0 to 1 (1.0:1).

CALCULATOR GUIDE

▶ 2430000 ÷ 2405000 = ◀ **1.010395** or 1.0 to 1

Capitalization

A company's *capitalization* shows its source of funding. It is found by adding together long-term debt, preferred stock, and common stockholders' equity.

Common stockholders' equity usually has three components:

● The common stock account (number of common shares outstanding × par value).

● The capital surplus account.

● Retained earnings (earned surplus).

Since net worth includes the preferred stock account and all three elements of the common stock account, we can arrive at capitalization by adding long-term liabilities and net worth.

Capitalization = Long-Term Liabilities + Net Worth

Example: See Figure 27-1.

Capitalization = Long-Term Liabilities + Net Worth
= \$1,000,000 + \$7,390,000
= \$8,390,000

Marobeth's capitalization is \$8,390,000.

Capitalization Ratios

The *capitalization ratios* show the percent of the company's total capitalization represented by:

- Common stock (the common stock ratio).
- Preferred stock (the preferred stock ratio).
- Bonds (the bond ratio).

The three ratios add to 100%.

Common Stock Ratio. The common stockholders' equity is divided by the company's total capitalization.

$$\text{Common Stock Ratio} = \text{Common Stockholders' Equity} \div \text{Total Capitalization}$$

Common stockholders' equity, however, has three components:

- The common stock account (number of common shares outstanding × par value).
- The capital surplus account.
- Retained earnings (earned surplus).

Common stock
Capital surplus
+ Retained earnings
Common stockholders' equity

Example: See Figure 27-1. What is Marobeth's common stock ratio?

- First calculate common stockholders' equity:

Common stock	$1,900,000
Capital surplus	300,000
Retained earnings	4,690,000
Common stockholders' equity	$6,890,000

- Then apply the formula:

$$\text{Common Stock Ratio} = \text{Common Stockholders' Equity} \div \text{Total Capitalization}$$
$$= \$6,890,000 \div \$8,390,000$$
$$= 82\%$$

The common stock ratio is 82%.

▶ 1900000 + 300000 + 4690000 ÷ 8390000 × 100
= ◀ **82.12157** or 82%

Preferred Stock Ratio. The *preferred stock ratio* shows the percent of the corporation's total capitalization represented by preferred stock.

$$\frac{\text{Preferred}}{\text{Stock Ratio}} = \frac{\text{Preferred}}{\text{Stock}} \div \frac{\text{Total}}{\text{Capitalization}}$$

Example: See Figure 27-1.

$$\frac{\text{Preferred}}{\text{Stock Ratio}} = \frac{\text{Preferred}}{\text{Stock}} \div \frac{\text{Total}}{\text{Capitalization}}$$
$$= \$500,000 \div \$8,390,000 = 6\%$$

The preferred stock ratio is 6%.

▶ 500000 ÷ 8390000 × 100 = ◀ **5.95947** or 6%

Bond Ratio. The bond ratio shows the percent of total capitalization represented by long-term debt.

$$\frac{\text{Bond}}{\text{Ratio}} = \frac{\text{Long-Term}}{\text{Liabilities (Bonds)}} \div \frac{\text{Total}}{\text{Capitalization}}$$

Example: See Figure 27-1.

$$\frac{\text{Bond}}{\text{Ratio}} = \frac{\text{Long-Term}}{\text{Liabilities (Bonds)}} \div \frac{\text{Total}}{\text{Capitalization}}$$
$$= \$1,000,000 \div \$8,390,000 = 12\%$$

Marobeth's bond ratio is 12%.

▶ 1000000 ÷ 8390000 × 100 = ◀ **11.91895** or 12%

The three capitalization ratios should add to 100%.

Example: In the three previous examples we arrived at:

Common stock ratio	82%
Preferred stock ratio	6%
Bond ratio	12%
	100%

Inventory Turnover Ratio

The *inventory turnover ratio* shows how many times the inventory is "turned over" (sold) during the year.

Inventory Turnover Ratio = Net Sales ÷ Inventory

Note: This computation is simplified; accountants would use a much more sophisticated technique.

Example: Refer to Figures 27-1 and 27-2.

$$
\begin{aligned}
\text{Inventory Turnover Ratio} &= \text{Net Sales} \div \text{Inventory} \\
&= \$14,488,000 \div \$2,115,000 \\
&= 6.85 \text{ X}
\end{aligned}
$$

The inventory turnover ratio for Marobeth is 6.85 X.

Figure 27-2

Marobeth Corporation Income Statement January 1–December 31, 1992	
Net Sales	$14,488,000
− Cost of Goods Sold	10,915,000
− Selling, General and	
Administrative Expenses	1,095,000
− Depreciation	886,000
Operating Income	1,592,000
+ Other Income	27,000
Total Income (EBIT)	1,619,000
− Interest on Bonds	90,000
− Taxes	509,000
Net Income	1,020,000
− Preferred Dividends	35,000
Net Earnings	$ 985,000

*Marobeth common stock is currently trading for 9⅞ and is paying an annual dividend of $0.08 per share.

CALCULATOR GUIDE

▶ 14488000 ÷ 2115000 = ◀ **6.8501182** or 6.85 X

Margin of Profit (Operating Ratio)

The *margin of profit,* or *operating, ratio* shows the percent of operating income to sales—how much is left after expenses.

Margin of Profit = Operating Income ÷ Net Sales

Example: Refer to Figure 27-2.

Margin of Profit = Operating Income ÷ Net Sales
                 = $1,592,000 ÷ $14,488,000 = 11%

Marobeth's margin of profit is 11%.

CALCULATOR GUIDE

▶ 1592000 ÷ 14488000 × 100 = ◀ **10.9884** or 11%

Expense Ratio

This is the "flip side" of the operating ratio. The *expense ratio* shows the percent of sales that were expended before arriving at operating income.

$$\text{Expense Ratio} = \frac{\text{Cost of Goods Sold} + \begin{array}{c}\text{Selling,}\\\text{General, and}\\\text{Administrative}\\\text{Expenses}\end{array} + \text{Depreciation}}{\text{Net Sales}}$$

Example: See Figure 27-2.

$$\text{Expense Ratio} = \frac{\text{Cost of Goods Sold} + \begin{array}{c}\text{Selling,}\\\text{General, and}\\\text{Administrative}\\\text{Expenses}\end{array} + \text{Depreciation}}{\text{Net Sales}}$$

$$= \frac{\$10,915,000 + \$1,095,000 + \$886,000}{\$14,488,000} = 89\%$$

CALCULATOR GUIDE

▶ 10915000 + 1095000 + 886000 ÷ 14488000 × 100
= ◀ **89.01159** or 89%

The two ratios, margin of profit and expense ratio, should add to 100%. We can check our last two calculations by adding them together:

Margin of Profit	11%
Expense Ratio	89%
	100%

Cash Flow

Since depreciation is a noncash expense, *cash flow* gives a truer picture of the company's actual cash position before dividends are paid.

Cash Flow = Net Income + Depreciation

Example: See Figure 27-2.

Cash Flow = Net Income + Depreciation
= $1,020,000 + $886,000 = $1,906,000

Cash flow for Marobeth is $1,906,000.

Earnings Per Share

Expressed as a dollar figure, *earnings per share* shows the company's results per share of common stock outstanding. It is sometimes called "earnings available for common stockholders" since it is calculated after all other expenses, including interest on bonds, taxes, and preferred dividend payments. It is calculated by dividing net earnings by the number of common shares outstanding.

$$\frac{\text{Earnings}}{\text{per Share}} = \text{Net Earnings} \div \frac{\text{Number of Common}}{\text{Shares Outstanding}}$$

To arrive at the number of common shares outstanding, see the balance sheet, specifically the Net Worth section. This shows the overall value of the company's common stock and its par value. To find out the number of common shares outstanding, divide the common stock account by the par value of the common shares.

$$\frac{\text{Common Stock}}{\text{Shares Outstanding}} = \frac{\text{Common Stock}}{\text{Account}} \div \text{Par Value}$$

Example: See Figures 27-1 and 27-2.

First find the number of shares of common stock outstanding. The common stock account in Figure 27-1 shows $1,900,000 and indicates a par value of $1 per share.

$$\frac{\text{Common Stock}}{\text{Shares Outstanding}} = \frac{\text{Common Stock}}{\text{Account}} \div \text{Par Value}$$
$$= \$1,900,000 \div \$1$$
$$= 1,900,000 \text{ shares}$$

Now you can calculate earnings per share. Figure 27-2 shows total net earnings of $985,000.

$$\frac{\text{Earnings}}{\text{per Share}} = \frac{\text{Total}}{\text{Net Earnings}} \div \frac{\text{Number of Common}}{\text{Shares Outstanding}}$$
$$= \$985,000 \div 1,900,000 = \$0.52 \text{ per share}$$

Marobeth's earnings per share are $0.52.

Earnings per Share Comparisons

To compare per-share earnings results on a year-to-year basis, do the following:

- Subtract the previous year's per-share earnings from the current year's per-share earnings.
- Divide by the previous year's figure.

$$\frac{\text{Per-Share}}{\text{Earnings}} = \frac{\text{Current Year's Earnings per Share} - \text{Previous Year's Earnings per Share}}{\text{Previous Year's Earnings per Share}}$$
$$\text{Comparison}$$

Example: Last year's per-share earnings were $0.40, and the current year's per-share earnings are $0.52 (see the previous example).

$$\begin{matrix} \text{Per-Share} \\ \text{Earnings} \\ \text{Comparison} \end{matrix} = \frac{\begin{matrix}\text{Current Year's} & \text{Previous Year's} \\ \text{Earnings per Share} - \text{Earnings per Share}\end{matrix}}{\text{Previous Year's Earnings per Share}}$$

$$= \frac{\$0.52 - \$0.40}{\$0.40} = +30\%$$

The company's per-share earnings were up 30% over the previous year's results.

CALCULATOR GUIDE

▶ 0.52 − 0.40 ÷ 0.40 × 100 = ◀ **30.** or 30%

Price/Earnings Ratio (P/E Ratio)

The *P/E ratio*—a most important ratio—shows the "multiple" of the per-share market price of the common stock compared with the stock's earnings per share. It shows by how many times the market price exceeds the earnings per share. It is used as a gauge of the relative "expensiveness" of the stock.

$$\text{P/E Ratio} = \frac{\text{Market Price}}{\text{per Share}} \div \frac{\text{Earnings}}{\text{per Share}}$$

Example: See Figure 27-2. The footnote to the income statement shows the current market price for the common stock to be 9⅞.

$$\text{P/E Ratio} = \frac{\text{Market Price}}{\text{per Share}} \div \frac{\text{Earnings}}{\text{per Share}}$$

Marobeth's P/E ratio is 19 X. The market price is 19 times the earnings per share.

CALCULATOR GUIDE

▶ 9.875 ÷ 0.52 = ◀ **18.990384** or 19 X

Payout Ratio

The percent of the earnings per share that the corporation pays out in common stock dividends is expressed by the *payout ratio*.

Payout Ratio = $\dfrac{\text{Dividend per}}{\text{Common Share}}$ ÷ $\dfrac{\text{Earnings per}}{\text{Common Share}}$

Example: See Figure 27-2. The footnote to the income statement shows the common stock's dividend per share to be $0.08. The earnings per share were calculated at $0.52 in a previous example.

Payout Ratio = $\dfrac{\text{Dividend per}}{\text{Common Share}}$ ÷ $\dfrac{\text{Earnings per}}{\text{Common Share}}$

           = $0.08 ÷ $0.52 = 15%

Marobeth pays out 15% of its earnings per share in dividends.

CALCULATOR GUIDE

▶ 0.08 ÷ 0.52 × 100 = ◀ **15.38461** or 15%

SELF-TEST

Use the balance sheet in Figure 27-3 and the income statement in Figure 27-4 for the Rizek Company to answer the Self-Test questions.

What is the Rizek Corporation's:

A. Working capital
B. Current Ratio
C. Quick Assets
D. Quick Asset Ratio
E. Total Capitalization
F. Common Stock Ratio
G. Preferred Stock Ratio
H. Bond Ratio
I. Inventory Turnover Ratio
J. Margin of Profit
K. Expense Ratio
L. Cash Flow
M. Earnings Per Share
N. Price/Earnings Ratio
O. Payout Ratio
P. If The Rizek Corporation earned $7.39 per share in 1991, how do this year's earnings compare, percentage-wise?

Figure 27-3

The Rizek Corporation
Balance Sheet
December 31, 1992

CURRENT ASSETS		CURRENT LIABILITIES	
Cash	$ 905,000	Dividends Payable	$ 835,000
Marketable Secs.	140,000	Accounts Payable	425,000
Accounts Rec.	3,645,000	Accrued Expenses	1,230,000
Inventory	3,890,000	Accrued Taxes	325,000
	8,580,000		2,815,000
		LONG-TERM LIABILITIES	
FIXED ASSETS		8% Bonds due 2001	3,500,000
Property & Plant	7,125,000	10% Bonds due 2005	2,500,000
Equipment	3,150,000		
Prepaid Expenses	1,000,000		
	11,275,000	TOTAL LIABILITIES	8,815,000

Figure 27-3 (continued)

INTANGIBLE ASSETS			
Goodwill	2,150,000		
		NET WORTH	
		8% Pfd. ($50 par)	1,000,000
		Common Stock ($5 par)	2,000,000
		Capital Surplus	800,000
		Retained Earnings	9,590,000
		TOTAL NET WORTH	13,390,000
TOTAL LIABILITIES			
TOTAL ASSETS	$22,005,000	AND NET WORTH	$22,005,000

Figure 27-4

The Rizek Corporation Income Statement January 1–December 31, 1992	
Net Sales	$37,450,000
– Cost of Goods Sold	29,345,000
– Selling, General and Administrative Expenses	1,200,000
– Depreciation	685,000
Operating Income	6,220,000
+ Other Income	165,000
Total Income (EBIT)	6,385,000
– Interest on Bonds	530,000
– Taxes	2,000,000
Net Income	3,855,000
– Preferred Dividends	80,000
Net Earnings	$3,775,000

*The Rizek Corporation's common stock is currently trading for 196½ per share and is paying an annual dividend of $4.25 per share.

ANSWERS TO SELF-TEST

A. $5,765,000

Current Assets – Current Liabilities
$8,580,000   – $2,815,000 = $5,765,000

B. 3 to 1

 Current Assets ÷ Current Liabilities
  $8,580,000 ÷ $2,815,000   = 3 to 1

C. $4,690,000

 Current Assets –   Inventory
  $8,580,000 – $3,890,000 = $4,690,000

D. 1.7 to 1

 Quick Assets ÷ Current Liabilities
  $4,690,000 ÷ $2,815,000   = 1.7 to 1

E. $19,390,000

 Long-Term Liabilities + Net Worth
      $6,000,000   + $13,390,000 = $19,390,000

(Both bond issues must be added when figuring long-term liabilities.)

F. 64%

Common Stockholders' Equity ÷ Total Capitalization
     $12,390,000   ÷ $19,390,000   = 64%

(Common stockholders' equity consists of common stock, capital surplus, and retained earnings.)

G. 5%

Preferred Stock ÷ Total Capitalization
 $1,000,000 ÷ $19,390,000   = 5%

H. 31%

   Bonds   ÷ Total Capitalization
$6,000,000 ÷ $19,390,000   = 31%

(Both bond issues must be added.)

Note: The three capitalization ratios total 100%.

Common Stock Ratio	64%
Preferred Stock Ratio	5%
Bond Ratio	31%
	100%

I. 9.6 X

 Net Sales   ÷   Inventory
$37,450,000 ÷ $3,890,000 = 9.6 X

J. 17%

Operating Income ÷   Net Sales
  $6,220,000   ÷ $37,450,000 = 17%

K. 83%

(Cost of Goods Sold
+ Selling, General and
Administrative Expenses ÷   Net Sales
   + Depreciation)
    $31,230,000   ÷ $37,450,000 = 83%

Note: The Margin of Profit (17%) and the Expense Ratio (83%) add to 100%.

L. $4,540,000

Net Income + Depreciation
$3,855,000 + $685,000 = $4,540,000

M. $9.44

Net Earnings ÷ Number of Common
Shares Outstanding
$3,775,000 ÷ 400,000 = $9.44

The number of common shares outstanding is determined by dividing the common stock account by the common stock's par value: $2,000,000 ÷ $5 = 400,000.

N. 21 X

Common Stock Price ÷ Earnings Per Share
$196.50 ÷ $9.44 = 21 X

O. 45%

Dividend Per Share ÷ Earnings Per Share
$4.25 ÷ $9.44 = 45%

P. + 28%

(1992 1991 1991
Earnings − Earnings) ÷ Earnings:
($9.44 − $7.39) ÷ $7.39 = + 28%

CHAPTER 28

TAX LOSS CARRYFORWARDS

Capital Gains and Losses

As of mid-1992, the tax implications were the same for both short-term and long-term gains and losses. Nevertheless, investors should distinguish between such gains and losses, and keep a separate listing for each.

No matter how actively an investor trades, only two figures need be maintained: (1) a net short-term amount and (2) a net long-term amount.

1. All *short-term trades* are netted out on a continuing basis.

Example: An investor sells a stock, creating a short-term gain of $500. She later sells another security, producing a short-term loss of $360. It is not necessary to keep a record of both the short-term gain and the short-term loss; all she has to do is net them out to a single short-term figure of a $140 gain (+ $500 gain − $360 loss = + $140 gain). If the investor then has a $450 short-term loss, she nets the previous balance of + $140 with the new loss of $450, to arrive at a new net figure of an overall short-term loss of $310 (+ $140 − $450 = − $310).

2. *Long-term gains and losses* are treated in a similar manner. Net all long-term transactions as they occur, so that you are carrying only a single net long-term figure, either a profit or a loss.

Example: An investor executes a number of trades in 1992, resulting in the following capital gains and losses. At year-end, what is the investor's net tax position?

1. January $ 500 short-term loss
2. March $1,250 long-term gain
3. April $2,350 short-term gain
4. May $ 800 short-term loss
5. July $3,150 short-term loss
6. September $ 900 long-term loss
7. October $4,350 long-term gain

At year-end, the investor has a net $2,100 short-term loss and a net $4,700 long-term profit. Here's what the investor's tax records should have shown just *after* each of the trades listed:

1. $ 500 short-term loss and no long term gain or loss.
2. $ 500 short-term loss and $1,250 long-term gain.
3. $1,850 short-term gain and $1,250 long-term gain.
4. $1,050 short-term gain and $1,250 long-term gain.
5. $2,100 short-term loss and $1,250 long-term gain.
6. $2,100 short-term loss and $ 350 long-term gain.
7. $2,100 short-term loss and $4,700 long-term gain.

The investor has both a (long-term) profit and a (short-term) loss.

When the investor ends the tax year with both a profit and a loss, the two figures are again netted out to reduce the final capital gains tax picture to a single number. This final number:

● Can be positive (a gain) or negative (a loss).
● Is *short term* if the short-term gains or losses exceed the long-term gains or losses.
● Is *long term* if the long-term gains or losses exceed the short-term gains or losses.

In other words, the final figure takes on the character of the larger of the two gains or losses.

Example: In the preceding example, the investor would report a net long-term gain of $2,600 for the entire tax year. This figure was arrived at by netting out the $2,100 short-term loss and the $4,700 long-term gain: − $2,100 + $4,700 = + $2,600. It's a long-term gain because the long-term gains exceeded the short-term losses.

If an investor has either both short- and long-term profits, or both short-and long-term losses, they are kept separate. The only situation in which short- and long-term transactions are netted together is when one is positive (a gain) and the other negative (a loss).

SELF-TEST

Show the investor's *final* reported capital gains figure(s) for each of the following situations.

A.	Short-term gain	$4,500
	Long-term loss	$1,250
B.	Short-term loss	$1,200
	Long-term gain	$3,000
C.	Short-term gain	$2,800
	Long-term loss	$3,500
D.	Short-term loss	$ 900
	Long-term gain	$ 300
E.	Short-term gain	$3,250
	Long-term gain	$1,500
F.	Short-term loss	$ 850
	Long-term loss	$1,500

ANSWERS TO SELF-TEST

A. Short-term gain of $3,250

B. Long-term gain of $1,800

C. Long-term loss of $700

D. Short-term loss of $600

E. Short-term gain of $3,250 *and* long-term gain of $1,500

F. Short-term loss of $850 *and* long-term loss of $1,500

Deduction of Capital Losses

Capital losses are deductible, within certain annual limits. Both short-term and long-term losses may be deducted, but short-term losses must be deducted before long-term losses. The annual maximum for deductible losses is $3,000— whether short-term, long-term, or some of each.

Whatever amount of losses exceeds the annual limit may be carried forward to be deducted in later years.

Example: An investor loses a total of $5,000 short-term in 1992. She is allowed to deduct $3,000 against ordinary income in 1992 and carry forward the balance of the loss, $2,000, to 1993. She begins 1993 with a short-term loss of $2,000. If she has no other capital gains and losses in 1993, she deducts the remaining $2,000 against her ordinary income.

Losses retain their short-term or long-term character when carried forward. Short-term loss carryforwards do not "age" to become long-term. Remember that short-term losses are to be used first.

Examples: Mr. Joseph Meehan ends the tax year with $490 in short-term losses. He deducts $490 from his ordinary income in that tax year. If Mr. Meehan had ended the tax year with $3,600 in short-term losses, he would deduct the maximum of $3,000 in the current year and carry forward the remaining $600 of short-term loss to the next year.

Mrs. Ernestine Sulton ended 1991 with long-term losses of $3,800. She may deduct $3,000 in 1991 and carry forward $800 as a long-term loss to 1992.

If Mrs. Sulton had total long-term losses of $7,500 in 1991, she would deduct $3,000 in 1991 and carry forward $4,500 to be used in subsequent years. If she had no other capital transactions in the next several years, she would deduct an additional $3,000 in 1992 and the remaining $1,500 in 1993. Thus she would deduct the entire loss of $7,500 spread over three tax years.

Steve Rizek ended 1991 with $900 in short-term losses and $3,500 in long-term losses. He may deduct all $900 of the short-term loss but only $2,100 of the long-term loss in 1991. He will thus have deducted the limit, $3,000, in 1991. This leaves Steve with a long-term tax loss carryforward of $1,400 ($3,500 − $2,100) for 1992.

If Steve had ended 1991 with $3,200 in short-term losses and $1,500 in long-term losses he would have deducted $3,000 of the short-term loss in 1991 and carried forward the remaining $200 of short-term loss and the entire $1,500 of long-term loss.

SELF-TEST

For each of the following year-end situations, show the deduction for the current tax year and the carryforward(s), if any, for subsequent years. Indicate whether the carryforwards are short-term or long-term losses.

A. Short-term loss of $2,000 and long-term loss of $3,850

B. Short-term loss of $3,500 and long-term loss of $4,000

C. Short-term gain of $450 and long-term loss of $5,400

D. Short-term loss of $2,500 and long-term loss of $3,500

E. Short-term loss of $800 and long-term loss of $1,500

ANSWERS TO SELF-TEST

A. Deduct $3,000, carry forward $2,850 long-term loss.

B. Deduct $3,000, carry forward $500 short-term and $4,000 long-term losses.

C. Deduct $3,000, carry forward $1,950 long-term loss (the short-term gain and the long-term loss net out to a long-term loss of $4,950).

D. Deduct $3,000, carry forward $3,000 long-term loss.

E. Deduct $2,300, no carryforwards.

A Final Word

The mathematics of the securities industry can be bewildering to the uninitiated, but it is second nature to the practiced. We urge you to review the formulas presented, as often as you need to, until you are able to apply them to real-world situations.

Those preparing for a successful taking of the stockbroker's (the series 7) exam *must* be able to answer the majority of the Self-Test questions correctly. Private investors are also well advised to master as much of the text as possible. They will be better able to monitor their investments, to read and understand the financial press, and to interact more professionally with their brokers and investment advisors.

Success in your investment endeavors!

INDEX OF FORMULAS

This index summarizes the calculations in the book, giving you examples in many cases. If you need further information, refer to the chapters themselves, for which page numbers are provided to the right.

$0.35 Quarterly Dividend =
$0.35 × 4   = $1.40 Annual Dividend Rate

5
Interest Payments   24

Par Value × Coupon Rate

$10,000 Par Value Bonds @ 9% Coupon =
$10,000 × 0.09   = $900 Annual Interest

6
Accrued Interest—
Corporate and Municipal Bonds   30

$$\text{Annual Interest} \times \frac{\text{Number of Days from Last Payment Through Day before Settlement}}{360}$$

$10,000 Par Value 9% bond
Interest Payment Dates: January and July 1
Sold May 2 for settlement May 9

$$\$900 \times \frac{\$128}{360} = \$320 \text{ accrued Interest}$$

Accrued Interest—Government Bonds and Notes

$$\frac{\text{Semiannual}}{\text{Interest}} \times \frac{\text{Number of Days from Last Payment Through Day before Settlement}}{\text{Number Days in the Trade's Half Year}}$$

$1,000,000 Par Value 8% Bonds
Interest Payment Dates: May and November 15
Sold June 3 for settlement June 4

$$\$40,000 \times \frac{20}{184} = \$4,347.83 \text{ accrued Interest}$$

7
Current Yield   39

Annual Dividend (or Interest) ÷ Current Price

Stock paying $1.20 annually and trading at 18⅞.
$1.20 ÷ 18.875 = 6.4% current yield

8
Nominal Yield   45

The same as the coupon rate

8% bonds have a nominal yield of 8.00%.

9
Yield-to-Maturity—Basis Pricing   48

The discount rate at which the present value of all future payments would equal the present price of the bond, assuming that coupons are reinvested at the yield to maturity. Found by using a "basis" book or an especially programmed calculator (see the yield-basis book in Chapter 9, and Chapter 10 for the Rule-of-Thumb Yield-to-Maturity).

The Yield-Basis Book—Interpretation and Interpolation

Basis books may be used (1) to determine a bond's true yield to maturity, given its current price, or (2) to figure the price of a bond, given its yield to maturity. To calculate a yield for a price between those listed in the basis book, set up a proportion. See text for details.

10
The Rule-of-Thumb Yield to Maturity   56

$$\frac{\text{Annual Interest or } + \dfrac{\text{Discount}}{\text{Years to Maturity}} - \dfrac{\text{Premium}}{\text{Years to Maturity}}}{(\text{Current Value} + 1{,}000) \div 2}$$

Bond with an 8% coupon, 10 years to maturity, priced @ 98

$$\frac{(80) + 20 \div 10}{(980 + 1{,}000) \div 2} = \frac{80 + 2}{1{,}980 \div 2} = \frac{82}{990} = 8.28\%$$

11
Pricing Municipal Bonds   62

Municipal bonds are priced either like corporate bonds (dollar bonds, see Chapter 2), or on a yield-to-maturity basis (see Chapters 9 and 10).

12
Comparing Tax-Free and Taxable Yields   67

$$\text{Tax-Exempt Yield} \div (1. - \text{Tax Bracket Percent}) = \text{Taxable Equivalent Yield}$$

Client in the 33% tax bracket holds a tax-free bond with a yield of 8.5% and wishes to know the yield she must receive from a taxable bond to receive the equivalent after-tax return.

$$8.50 \div (1. - 0.33) = 8.50 \div 0.67 = 12.69\% \quad \text{Taxable Equivalent Yield}$$

13
Pricing Treasury Bills: Discount Yields, Coupon Equivalent Yields

Treasury bills are priced on a discounted yield basis. Converting the quotations into dollar prices is a two-step process:

$$\text{Discount} = \frac{\text{Par Value} \times \text{Price}}{\text{(decimal form)}} \times \frac{\text{Days to Maturity}}{360}$$

Then: Par Value − Discount = Dollar Price

What is the dollar price for $1,000,000 Treasury bills maturing in 95 days and trading at 5.42?

$$\$1,000,000 \times 0.0542 \times \frac{95}{360} = \$14,302.78 \quad \text{(discount)}$$

$$\$1,000,000 - \$14,302.78 = \$985,697.30 \quad \text{(dollar price)}$$

To convert to a coupon-equivalent yield:

$$\frac{\text{Discount}}{\text{Dollar Price}} \times \frac{365}{\text{Days to Maturity}} = \frac{\text{Coupon-Equivalent}}{\text{Yield}}$$

$$\frac{\$14,302.78}{\$985,697.30} \times \frac{365}{95} = 5.58\%$$

14
Pricing Mutual Funds

$$\frac{\text{Total}}{\text{Market Price}} = \frac{\text{Number of}}{\text{Fund Shares Held}} \times \frac{\text{Bid}}{\text{Price}}$$

GibOp has a per-share bid price of 11.54. An investor owns 500 shares.

500 shares × $11.54 = $5,770

15
Mutual Funds

Net Asset Value Per Share (Bid Price)

$$\frac{\text{Total Assets} - \text{Total Liabilities}}{\text{Number of Shares Outstanding}}$$

ABC mutual fund has 1,586,000 shares outstanding, total assets of $13,365,000, and total liabilities of $2,013,000.

$$\frac{\$13,365,000 - \$2,013,000}{1,586,000 \text{ per share}} = \$7.16 \text{ net asset Value}$$

Offering Price

$$\frac{\text{Net Asset Value}}{1. - \text{Percent Sales Charge}}$$

The Treanor Fund has a sales charge of 7% and a net asset value of $13.65.

$$\frac{\$13.65}{1. - 0.07} \quad \frac{\$13.65}{0.93} = \$14.68 \text{ offering Price}$$

Sales Charges

$$\frac{\text{Maximum Sales Charge}}{(\text{as a Percent of the offer Price})} = \frac{\text{Offer Price} - \text{Bid Price}}{\text{Offer Price}}$$

The Chirico Fund is quoted 20.24—22.12.

$$\frac{22.12 - 20.24}{22.12} = \frac{1.88}{22.12} = 8.5\% \text{ (sales charge)}$$

Redemption Fees

$$\frac{\text{Redemption}}{\text{Value}} = \frac{(\text{Number of}}{\text{Shares} \times \text{NAV})} \times \frac{(1. - \text{Percent}}{\text{Redemption Fee})}$$

The Lemel Fund has a net asset value (NAV) per share of $19.39 and levies a redemption fee of 1%. A client redeeming 1,200 shares would receive:

$$(1,200 \times \$19.39) \times (1. - 0.01) = \$23,268 \times 0.99$$
$$= \$23,035.32$$

Breakpoint Sales

The sales charge is reduced for certain amounts of "bulk" purchases such as $10,000 or $25,000.

The Cartlidge Fund has a maximum sales charge of 8.5%, which reduces to 7.5% for purchases of $10,000 to $24,999. The fund is quoted 18.85—20.60. If Claudette Morgan purchases $12,500 of the fund, how many shares will she receive?

The offering price of 20.60 applies only to purchases at the maximum sales charge (8.5%). Miss Morgan's purchase will be made at the 7.5% level:

$$\frac{18.85}{1. - 0.075} = \frac{18.85}{0.925} = \$20.38$$

$$\$12,500 \div \$20.38 \qquad = 613.346 \text{ shares}$$

Right of Accumulation

Once a breakpoint has been reached through previous purchases, all *future* purchases are made at the reduced breakpoint level.

16
Rights Offerings   89

Stock trading without rights (ex rights):

$$\text{Theoretical Value of a right} = \frac{\text{Market Price} - \text{Subscription Price}}{\text{Number of Rights Needed to Subscribe (stock trading ex-rights)}}$$

Stock trading with rights (cum-rights):

$$\text{Theoretical Value of a right} = \frac{\text{Market Price} - \text{Subscription Price}}{\text{Number of Rights Needed to Subscribe} + 1 \text{ (stock trading cum-rights)}}$$

MNO is offering new shares on a four-for-one basis at 34 per share. MNO's "old" stock is trading at 30, ex-rights.

$$\frac{34 - 30}{4} = 1 \text{ (theoretical value of a right)}$$

PQR is offering new shares on a six-for-one basis at 85 per share. PQR's "old" stock is trading at 82, cum-rights.

$$\frac{85 - 82}{6 + 1} = \$0.43 \text{ (theoretical value of a right)}$$

17
Convertible Securities   93

Conversion Price

Convertible securities are described as being convertible "at" a specific price. This price, divided into the convertible security's par value, gives the number of common shares into which the security is convertible (the conversion *ratio*).

XYZ convertible preferred is convertible at $50 and has a par value of $100 per share. XYZ convertible preferred has a conversion *price* of $50 and a conversion *ratio* of 2.

$$(100 \div 50 = 2)$$

Each share of preferred may be exchanged for 2 shares of common stock.

Conversion Ratio

The number of shares of common stock to be received in exchange for a convertible preferred stock or bond.

See previous section for method of changing conversion price to conversion ratio.

Parity

When a convertible security and its underlying common stock are in equilibrium.

Convertible bonds are exchangeable for 50 shares of RFQ common stock. The bonds are trading at 105⅝ and the stock at 21⅛. The bond is selling for $1,056.25 and is exchangeable for exactly that same dollar value of common stock.

50 shares of the common stock at 21⅛ also equal $1,056.25 (50 × 21.125 = 1,056.25).

The convertible bond and the common stock into which it is convertible are said to be trading "at parity."

Arbitrage

When a convertible security is trading at a discount to parity with its underlying stock, there is an opportunity to simultaneously buy the convertible security and sell the underlying stock, thereby locking in a profit. These opportunities are very rare and are almost immediately taken advantage of by professional arbitragers.

Refer to the previous section on Parity. If the bonds were trading at 103 rather than 105⅝, it would be possible to buy the bond for $1,030 and simultaneously sell the underlying 50 shares of stock at 21⅛. The sale of stock would bring in $1,056.25, which gives the arbitrager a profit (ignoring commissions) of $26.25 per bond.

"Forced" Conversion

When a convertible issue is called, the owner must determine whether the market value of stock to be received upon conversion exceeds the call price. If he/she would receive *more* by converting just prior to the call rather than accepting the call, it is known as a "forced" conversion.

MNO convertible bonds are exchangeable for 34 shares of MNO common stock. MNO announces that they are calling the bonds at 102. The common stock is trading at 31⅜. If the bondholder accepts the call (does not convert), he will receive $1,020 in cash. If he does convert, he will receive 34 shares of common stock worth $1,066.75 (34 × 31⅜). Thus, he is "forced" to convert in order to realize the larger dollar value.

18
Bond Amortization and Accretion   99

The "tax-cost" basis of many bonds changes over time. When the basis price of a bond purchased at a premium is lowered over time, it is known as *amortization*. Raising the basis price over time for a bond purchased at a discount is known as *accretion*.

A bond with 10 years remaining to maturity is purchased at 104½. What is the bond's cost basis after being held 5 years?

The bond was purchased for $1,045—a premium of $45. This $45 premium is amortized over the life of the bond so that, every year to maturity, the "cost" of the bond is reduced by 1/10 of the premium, or $4.50. After the bond is held 5 years, the "cost" of the bond is reduced to $1,022.50 ($1,045 − [5 × $4.50] = $1,045 − $22.50 = $1,022.50).

Accretion (raising the cost basis) is figured in a similar fashion.

19
Basic Margin Transactions   102

Equity in a *long* account:

Long Market Value − Debit Balance = Equity

Equity in a *short* account:

Credit Balance − Short Market Value = Equity

Margin Calls

Margin calls are generated only when a position is established or increased (long purchases or short sales). The current requirement (Regulation T) is 50%.

20
Excess Equity and the Special Memorandum Account (SMA)   107

When the equity in a margin account exceeds the requirement, the "excess" equity is transferred to the SMA. Such excess equity, within certain limits, can be used to purchase additional securities without putting up additional cash, or may be sent to the client in cash. Either use of the SMA will increase the account's debit balance.

Buying Power

The dollar value of securities that may be purchased in a margin account without the client having to send in additional money. The buying power is *twice* the value of the SMA.

Cash Available

The amount of cash that may be sent to the owner of a margin account. It is equal to the SMA, provided that the cash payment does not reduce the account's equity below either 25% of market value or $2,000.

22
Margin: Maintenance Requirements for Long Accounts   120

For long accounts the maintenance requirement is 25%.

23
Margin: Maintenance Requirements for Short Accounts   125

The short account maintenance requirement varies with the price of the short position:

Price of Short Stock	Maintenance Requirement
0–2½	$2.50 per share
2½–5	100%
5–16⅝	$5.00 per share
16¾ or higher	30%

Maintenance Calls

Maintenance calls for long accounts may be met by:

● A deposit of cash in the amount of the call.

● A deposit of marginable securities with a market value of 133% of the amount of the call.

● A sellout of securities in the account having a market value of 4 times the amount of the call.

24
Margin: Maintenance Excess   130

Maintenance excess is the amount by which a margin account's equity exceeds the account's maintenance requirement.

25
Pricing Options   132

Equity options: Priced in points and eighths of points, like stocks. Lower-priced options may trade in sixteenths.

Debt options: The currently active debt options (options on short-term and long-term interest rates traded on the CBOE) trade in points, eighths, and sixteenths like equity options.

Foreign currency options: Premiums, strike prices, and underlying currency values are expressed in cents or hundredths of cents.

Index options: Traded in points, eighths, and sixteenths, like stock options.

26
Options Margin   141

Stock options: 20% of Underlying + Premium

Debt options (for CBOE short-term and long-term interest rates): 10% of Underlying + Premium

    See text for T-notes and bonds.

Foreign currency options: 4% of Underlying + Premium

Index options (broad-based): 15% of Index Value
                         + Premium
            (narrow-based): 20% of Index Value
                         + Premium

Note: The figure for each of the above may be reduced by the amount by which the margined option is out-of-the-money, except that the lower limit to which it may be reduced is:

Equity options	10% minimum
Debt options	5% minimum
Foreign currency options	0.75% minimum
Index options	10% minimum

27
Financial Ratios   147

Working Capital = Current Assets − Current Liabilities

Current Ratio = Current Assets ÷ Current Liabilities

Quick Asset Ratio = Quick Assets − Current Liabilities

Capitalization = Bonds + Net Worth

$$\text{Common Stock Ratio} = \frac{\text{Common Stock} + \text{Capital Surplus} + \text{Retained Earnings}}{\text{Capitalization}}$$

Preferred Stock Ratio = Preferred Stock ÷ Capitalization

Bond Ratio = Bonds ÷ Capitalization

Inventory Turnover Ratio = Sales ÷ Inventory

Margin of Profit = Operating Income ÷ Sales

$$\text{Expense Ratio} = \frac{\text{Cost of Goods Sold} + \text{Selling General, and Administrative Expenses} + \text{Depreciation}}{\text{Sales}}$$

Cash Flow = Net Income + Depreciation

Earnings/Share = Net Earnings ÷ Number of Common Shares Outstanding

$$\text{Price/Earnings Ratio} = \frac{\text{Market Price/Share}}{\text{Earnings/Share}}$$

Payout Ratio = Dividend/Share ÷ Earnings/Share

28
Tax Loss Carryforwards

Investors may only deduct, from ordinary income, a maximum of $3,000 of *net* losses in a single tax year.

Any net losses greater than the $3,000 annual limit may be carried forward to subsequent tax years.

Short-term losses are used first, then long-term losses.

Index